ABUSED...

ABANDONED...

STILL STANDING

The Autobiography

of Ruby Davis

Abused... Abandoned... Still Standing

Copyright © 2009 Ruby J. Davis

ISBN: 978-1-935125-28-0

Book printed in the United States of America

To order additional copies of this book go to:
www.rp-author.com/Davis

Rp

Robertson Publishing
59 N. Santa Cruz Avenue, Suite B
Los Gatos, California 95030 USA
(888) 354-5957 • www.RobertsonPublishing.com

DEDICATION

This book is dedicated to all the beautiful women in the world that GOD has created. Those who have been abused, abandoned, misused and disrespected by men that, in other words, are victims of Domestic Violence. The woman who did everything she could but he still didn't appreciate her and used her for a punching bag. If he left you for another women, don't be disappointed just remember he will be doing the same thing to her. I know people made you feel like you were worthless and nobody else wanted you, but hold on, don't give up, GOD can turn things around for you the same way He did it for me. Everything that a man has done to you, will be done to him. Take this as a learning experience and use it for your own benefit because if GOD allows you to live through it, though many of us don't, it will make you more of a woman than you can imagine.

Women, it is time for us to wake up, stand up and be ourselves because we aren't supposed to find good men, they are supposed to find us. Life is beautiful and we are supposed to live it to the fullest but we must realize that no one can stop us but us. Don't do to others what you don't want to be done to you. D.V.I.R. Domestic Violence Is Real, don't be a victim, because you don't have to be.

R. U. B.Y

Rise

Up

Be

Yourself

TABLE OF CONTENTS

ACKNOWLEDGMENTS

TO GOD

For creating me exactly the way He did and accepting me the way I am.

My Father and Mother (deceased)

To both my parents (*Clarence and Macola Bramlett*) if it wasn't for them and their prayers I would not be the person that I am today. What my parents taught me has motivated me and encouraged me to realize that I can do all things through Christ, who strengthens me. Although my parents have completed their journey here on earth every day, when I look in the mirror, I can see them in me and this is what makes me strive to be the best that I can be. I try to live by the principles that they taught me, don't do to anyone what you don't want them to do to you. Last but not least I thank them for believing in me even when I did not believe in myself.

My Children

To my wonderful children; my son *Sammie Wright Jr.* and my daughter *Kathyrn Macol Johnson*. They are truly blessings from GOD. I can't explain the love that a mother has for her own children, ones she carried next to her heart for nine long months. I do realize that the struggles and difficult challenges we have had to endure has caused us to be apart for quite sometime, but GOD is going to allow everything to work for our good. It is because of both of you that I strive to do the best I can and be all that I can. It is because of you that I can stand up and be me. Even after all the difficult times we have gone through we still have each other and no matter what, I will always be your mother and you will always be my children. That is something that no one can take away from us.

Grandchildren

To *Tameka*, the mother of my grandchildren. I can't recognize my grandchildren without recognizing you. Thank you for having them. This is what every mother wishes to live to see. I realize that if it wasn't for you they would not be here.

Samojha Lee Wright (deceased)

Pay'd Lee Wright

Sammie Lee Wright III

Me and My Children

Me and My Grandchildren

My Son and His Sons

Me, My Children, Grandchildren and Daughter-In-Law

A SPECIAL THANKS TO

My Mother-in-Law

Mattie Jackson for taking me under your roof and not making me go back home when I was so young.

Nathaniel Williams (deceased)

For opening my eyes to GOD and making me realize that I am somebody who deserves better.

My Children's Fathers & Stepmothers

Sammie Wright Sr. and Linda. A special thanks to Sammie for stepping up to the plate to take care of your son the way that a father should do (when the mother is not capable or financially able). You have been in your son's life from day one and you chose to keep it that way. Thank you for that. I will always love you with the love of GOD. I am aware that it also takes a good women by your side to make this possible. A special thanks to you Linda, because you didn't have to do the things that you did for my son. It was his father's responsibility. Thank you.

Maurice Johnson and Bobbie. Maurice you missed out on many years of Kathyrn's life — from two years old to fifteen and half years old. As we know these are years you can't get back. Please embrace the moments that you have with your daughter right now, it is not about me nor is it about you, it is about her. Life is short — enjoy the time you have with her. She has waited all her life to actually have an opportunity to be with her father, so please just be her father and don't mistreat her, everything else will fall into place. You have only had her a little over a year and this is a critical time in her life. You are an influence in her life right now because you are her role model. At this point you will either make her love you or hate you, the choice is yours. You have missed out on quite a few years of her life and GOD has given you the opportunity to be her father now, so stand up and be her father, no one ever said it was going to be easy. It was never easy for me as a single mother with her, so don't expect things to be easy. I also realize that it takes a good women by your side to make this possible, a special thanks to you Bobbie because you didn't have to do the things that you did for my daughter. It is her father's responsibility. Thank you.

INTRODUCTION

You Never Miss Your Water Until The Water Fountain Runs Dry.

I am truly blessed, I was born and raised in a two parent Christian home, both parents living for GOD. My mother and father had six kids together, one boy and five girls. I am next to the youngest, considered back in the day as the knee (lap) baby. We lived a very simple but quality life. We would go to Church on Sundays and the rest of the days were all about the family. My father worked outside the home and my mother was a stay-at-home mom, which I can now identify as the most challenging work that one can have.

Every morning mom cooked a hot breakfast for the family and prepared dad's box lunch. Every morning before school Mom made sure all five girl's hair was combed and that we never missed the school bus. At home education was a must. Every day after school there was always a hot meal awaiting for the children and a hot supper for my dad. On Saturdays my parents would shop for the week and get any groceries and supplies that were needed for the home.

My father was a genuine man. He made sure his wife and kids got everything they needed. Church was the center of our life, that was never an option. My dad would always stress to us how GOD looked at our heart and not the outside, he also added that people would turn their back on you, even your own family. Dad also noted that true friends, for the most part, don't really exist. As you go through life you will see exactly what I mean. My father's favorite words were *"Just keep on living and you will see"*.

This was our life, and what a wonderful life this was, and in just one night I made the conscience choice to throw it all away.

Chapter 1

Growing Up

I was born and raised in the Delta of Mississippi first in a small town on a dirt road called Blue Lake. Later, when I was 6 years old, my father had the family house built from the ground up in a subdivision called Goose Pond. A country girl as one might say bare foot, dirt road, chopping cotton in the summer time etc. but as I look back those were the days that taught us how to get up and go to work. Those were the days that prepared us, so that we could later be on our own and not have to depend on someone else.

I've always felt that my father was a mean man because his rules were firm and in most cases there was never an option. I have always been a thinker, trying to figure out things and the reasons behind them. At times I felt like I was in the wrong place because I always felt that there had to be a better way of living in the world. I always had bigger dreams and wanted to do so much more than what I was experiencing in the country. I got tired of going to the cotton field every summer. It was never an option because once we were of age we had to go to the cotton field. I was tired of seeing so many black people afraid of white people as well. I felt that life wasn't supposed to be like that, everyone was human so why were we treated so differently? Was it just because we were black? I never could understand that concept for some reason.

I would always observe the things that my mom did on a daily basis how she made things seem so easy to do. Sewing, cooking, doing our hair. By the time I was three or four years old I was making dolls clothes and braiding the dolls hair as well. As the years passed I was braiding, pressing and curling everyone's hair in the

1

family at an early age. My mom would always tell me that I was going to be a beautician and she said I can do anything that I put my mind too. For some reason my mom would always treat me differently than my siblings and I never knew why. No matter what the situation was my mother always had a way of making me laugh until tears rolled down my face.

I became a teenager and of course I thought that I was a grown-up because I was just as big as my older siblings. I had watched my mom take care of the entire household my entire life and she made it seem really simple. One of my dreams was to be happily married and committed to my kids just like my mom. I felt that I could do this on my own someday. I wanted to have a life like my mom had, and married to a good man like my father. My father always stood up and did whatever it took to take care of his wife and children.

My parents were such good role models because they taught us good moral values and how to be responsible. They also taught us how we should treat people, the way we wanted to be treated, and would always inform us that what goes around comes back around. In other words, they taught us to make sure we did the right thing at all times. At times mom would talk to us about life and would also stress how wonderful and respectful it was to have a husband and not just sleeping around with different men. She always said that wasn't nice and it wasn't lady like to deal with more than one man at a time. It was an extreme disgrace for the woman and it will give her a bad name. She also stated that one man was more than enough, just settle down and have your family. I felt that I could that be married and committed to one man as long as the both of us loved each other and wanted the same thing in life.

As time went on I had started playing with the boys at school and I really liked one of them. Even before getting to high school I would see him at school every day, and he would constantly play with me. I had seen him at school a couple of years before we exchanged telephone numbers. Eventually he asked me for my phone number and I gave it to him and he gave me his. My parents were not fond of us talking on the phone especially to boys but I would sneak and call him every chance I got. My father always told us that talking on the telephone was a waste of time and energy and the person on the other end did not mean us any good, especially the boys. He wanted us to go to school and just focus on our education because he knew we were going to need it someday. He also knew boys would just come and go and it would not mean a thing. My father stated, "All that the boys want is to give you a house full of babies and leave you." We as kids would hear that but would not believe that this could happen to us. This also did not change my mind about wanting to be with boys because I figured that not all of them could be the same way.

My parents were very strict on all of us, which led to curiosity about some things in life. We were called the church girls because that was the only place we actually went to, other than school. There were a lot of things that my parents never talked about with us so therefore we just had to learn a lot of things on our own. They would not allow us to do hardly anything and most of the time there wasn't a reason why we couldn't do it, so this left a lot of curiosity in my mind.

I had become fond of one of the boys at school and would see him every day and of course he pretended that he liked me very much. But I noticed that he would chase behind almost every other girl at the school as well. This was a red flag, but I was young and naive and didn't pay attention to the signs that were right before my eyes. Of course he would tell me that the other girls didn't mean anything to him and I was the only one he really wanted to be with. I didn't know any better and I thought he really meant that.

There were many times when I felt left out when I was at home with my family. It made me feel as though I wasn't good enough and nobody really cared for me. There are times when siblings can treat and act mean toward one another and they are not even aware of your feeling at all. This could be the way that teenagers are supposed to act, who knows. I could easily tell when people didn't really want me around. I have always been like that as long as I can remember. I had three sisters older than me and one sister younger than me but where did I fit in? I never knew everyone was so different and that you never knew if they really wanted you around or not. I think this might be one of the biggest problems for many families, not realizing and being able to accept that everyone is different and think differently. We spend so much time trying to change people but this is not our job, only GOD can change people. Everyone always feels that nothing is wrong with them, it is always the other person that has the problem and not them. Although everyone is different and thinks differently it does not make a person crazy, it makes them unique. This is how GOD created us, everyone is uniquely designed exactly the way GOD wanted them to be so if you are not pleased with yourself, take it out on GOD not other people. Everyone is not always going to do things the way that people think they should be done. Sometimes it can be so hard to accept people the way they are but we have to keep in mind that just because they are different, act different and do things differently it doesn't make them a bad person nor a foolish person. It only means that they are different from you. After feeling like an outcast it only made me more eager to leave and be on my own. The bottom line is I wanted to be grown and on my own. Everyone knows that nothing just happens, everything is thought out and planned out before action is actually taken.

It was 1984. Sam and I had been talking for some time now and we plotted a way for me to run away from home to be with him. As soon as I felt that I was ready and the time was right this was exactly what I did. As soon as school was out in the summer of 1984 we had already planned what we was going to do, when and how it was going to take place. I had been gradually packing some of my clothes and personal items that I would need for the getaway. As time got closer I was getting kind of afraid but I knew this is what I wanted to do. Something inside of me was telling me this is what I needed to do and the time had come. I felt that this was my only opportunity to get away. Being that I was about fifteen years old, and a minor, I knew doing it the right way would never work because my parents would never agree to that.

So one Saturday night around midnight, when I knew my entire family would be asleep in bed, my bag was in the guest room, packed, all set and ready to go. I had already talked to Sam earlier that night and we had confirmed everything that was going to take place. I went into the guest room and locked the door behind me and of course Sam was at the window waiting for me. I went to the closet, got my bag, and out the window I went. Everything went according to the way we had planned it. Not even a second thought about what would happen when the morning came. Being as young as I was and not really knowing the meaning of true love I really thought that I had found someone that really loved me and we would be together the rest of our lives.

We spent the entire summer running and hiding, so my family would not find me and make me come back home. I did not want to go back home, my father had put so much fear in us I knew what was going to happen and how I was going to be treated if I went back home. I knew my father was going to beat me like crazy and I didn't want to go through that. I never stopped to think how running away from home might have affected my family. I figured they didn't love me anyway so it wouldn't matter if I were there or not. This was how I was feeling deep down inside.

Finally after months and months had gone by I decided to show my face and see my family. When I saw the look on their faces I realized that there is no way I could go back home — it will never be the same. My mother stressed how important it was for me to keep going to school so I could finish high school. She would always tell me, "Make sure you finish high school because you are going to need an education to make it in life." She always told us that my father never finished school because he had to work and she didn't get a chance to finish school either. I promised her that I would complete school. I never intended to quit school, I always knew that I had to finish high school. I also wanted to go to college as well. My parents believed in education and this was something that I wanted to continue to do as well because I loved school. My plan was never just to leave home and do nothing, I wanted to leave home because I felt that life had more to offer than what I was experiencing in Mississippi.

My goal was have a better life and to succeed in life. So my parents wanted to make sure that everyone finished school and went on to college. She said in the years to come we would need a college education in order to get good jobs. My mother taught me to always finish what I started, and never leave anything undone. After showing my face my family realized that I was with a boy named Sam. It was no longer a secret that I had run away from home to be with him. I gave up everything to be with Sam. When school started in the fall Sam's mother took me in and enrolled me in school so that I could continue my schooling and not get behind. However, Sam had already decided not to go to school and continued to work because he had to take care of me. He had to make sure that I got all the things I needed in order to go to school. His mother would not allow us to live together because we weren't married yet. Sam stayed with his grandparents and he would come visit me every weekend. Sam was taking care of me because his mother had told him that I was his responsibility from now on. None of Sam's family tried to make me go back home. We lived in a small town and everyone had heard how mean my father was. My father was the type of man that nobody bothered in no kind of way, not even the white men, because they were afraid of him. He was just the type of person that didn't let anyone run over him, he stood up to everyone. He stood up for what he believed was right.

Sam and I made plans to relocate to Springfield Illinois during Christmas break while school was out. Sam and I went to visit my parents for the very first time together. I think Sam was afraid of my father but he tried not to show it. I could tell by the look on my father's face that he was not pleased at all with the decision that we both had made. My father was calm he didn't really have anything to say and I think everyone had gotten used to me not being at home anymore. I had been gone about six months and due to me leaving the way I did many had things changed at home. I believe my father also realized that being so strict on us did not keep us from doing what we really wanted to do. What it did was make us want to do it even more. My father, being the man that he was, knew that Sam was not going to do the right thing by me. I could tell that he was disappointed in the choice that I had made, to change my entire life, but he did not try to stop me. He knew I wanted to live my own life and would face trials and tribulations that I knew nothing about. My father had been very strict on everyone by not letting us have any freedom at all and I had three older sisters and he really wasn't allowing them to date or anything. So I knew I would not stand a chance in dating any time soon. We had only gone to visit my parents to let them know that we would be moving to Springfield Illinois. We'd stay with Sam's family until we got our own place. I didn't have any relatives there at all but it didn't matter to me as long as I was with Sam. It didn't matter where we went, I just knew I didn't want to go back home. I could tell that my father was not pleased but he knew I was going to Springfield whether they gave me permission or not. My father believed that it would never work out well and that Sam was not going to treat me right because it all started out wrong and it would end wrong. Deep down inside he had to have known that I could make it, because he didn't try to convince me not to go. I felt good when I departed from my family at that particular time to move to Springfield, Illinois. My mother always showed me love no matter what choices I decided to make. I really didn't feel like I was hurting anyone when I left because I felt that no one wanted me around and this was my opportunity to get away. My mother already knew I could make it but she also knew I had to go through my own trials and tribulations and nobody ever knows what that is going to be. No one can tell you what is actually set before you in life.

The very next day Sam and I caught the greyhound bus to Springfield Illinois. We sat on the front seat like two little kids relocating to have a better life together. I did not have a clue of the changes that was about to happen in my life. This move was like jumping out of the skillet into the frying pan and I had no idea. I never saw any of it coming. The entire time I'd spent with Sam I had only seen one side of him, which was his good side, and that was all I knew.

Chapter 2

Life with Sam

After arriving in Springfield, Illinois, my whole life changed. Sam and I were both still too young to do things on our own. Sam's aunt became my guardian and enrolled me in school. I was living a married life with a husband during my high school years and I never thought anything different of it. Sam made sure I got to school every day and after school I would always do my homework. I enjoyed babysitting for my aunt-in-law and was having a ball. Sam had already found a job and for a while nothing seemed any different to me. Then as time went own Sam started going out with some buddies that he'd met at work and some cousins of his as well. Sam began to change. He starting showing me a side of him that I never thought could have existed. Then he started staying out late, we started having arguments, and begin fighting each other.

We had moved to Springfield, Illinois in December 1984 and in January 1985 Sam started hitting me. I would always hit him back. I thought it was just a joke at first. I never thought that this was going to turn out to be an abusive marriage and I would be a victim of domestic violence. Domestic violence was only something that I saw on TV shows. We had also found our own place as well and everything was happening so fast. I really didn't know that couples fought like that, I had never heard of such foolish thing. I was never in an environment like that. I was quickly exposed to a side of the world that I had no knowledge of and everybody was involved in. Drinking, drugs, clubs, gambling and parties was the name of the game. My whole lifestyle changed, everybody believed in party, party, you hardly ever heard the word Church except for some holidays and funerals. I was introduced to and took a part in everything that could become an addiction. I was getting into clubs as twenty one and I was still a teenager. I continued to go to school and my mother would write me almost every week and tell me that she loved me and she'd send me a dollar so I could write her back. My mother would always let me know that no matter what she still loved me.

By the time I was seventeen years old I had gone through so much as a teenager with Sam — it was unbelievable. I was a victim of domestic violence and I was tired of the fights, name calling, women, going back and forth to the emergency rooms, lying to the doctors, not being honest about my injuries. At the age of seventeen I tried moved back home with my parents so that I could complete my last year of high school. I thought that when I moved back home that everything would be the same as it was before I left, because I thought family would always be like family. I guess everyone changes over time, even family, but I never knew. My dad always told us people change. I never told my family about how abusive Sam was to me, that was a secret part of my life when it came to my family. I don't know if my family knew or not that I was getting beat down on a regular bases. Sam's entire family knew because most of them lived in Springfield and they witnessed most of the fights. I can remember when I moved back home my baby sister asked me, "How did that scar get in your eye?" When my baby sister ask me, the first thing I said was, "What scar?" knowing that I had almost lost my entire eye but GOD saved it.

It was late on one Saturday night and Sam had gone out with his buddies and had gotten extremely drunk (this was always his alibi). I was home babysitting his little cousins as usual. It was a night I will never forget, Sam came home and he was in such a rage. I don't really know what had happen to him, because I had not been with him, but he must have tried some type of new drug. But that night he could have killed me. I was lying home in bed in nothing but my night clothes, he was in such a rage and starting just arguing and fighting. As I was trying to get away he woke up everyone in the house but there was nothing that anyone could do but scream and cry. Sam jumped on me, bite me in my eye, and it started swelling rapidly. I could feel tears and rupture of vessels. I could hardly see anything. Trying to get away seemed impossible. I remember him locking me in the bathroom, pulling the rods off the bathroom walls and just threatening and beating me.

We finally got in bed and I tried to wait until he was asleep so I could run for help. He had already snatched the phone out of the wall so calling for help was not an option. Every time I moved he would wake up and tell me I wasn't going anywhere or he was going to kill me. I had a swollen face from the eye injury. Bruises were all over my body and there was nothing that I could do. I knew he was extremely drunk and at some point he would be knocked out for the rest of the morning but I didn't know when. I was devastated. I could not move, all I could think of is, when he goes to sleep I have to run for help because I knew my eye had been terribly injured. It didn't seem like he was ever going to go to sleep and I could feel that my eye had gotten so huge. I could hardly see a thing but I was going to make my getaway as soon as he passed out. Every time I moved, he moved. He kept his hands on me so when I did move he would know it and he could stop me. This was one of the longest nights of my life, it seemed like it would never end. Sam and I fought on a regular bases but he had never gone to those extremes, to almost kill me like that. Only GOD knows what else he did to me in the meantime before he finally passed out.

Eventually I was able to get up and ease out of the house just as I was, without getting anything. This man was crazy and I felt I had to run for my life, there was no time to think about getting dressed. It was early in the morning. I could remember hearing cars blowing their horns at me because I only had on my nightgown and house shoes. I must have been walking in and out of the streets. Nobody knew I could hardly see a thing. They probably wondered why was I in my nightgown and house shoes but I didn't care I needed help as soon as possible. Only GOD knows how I was able to walk almost three miles or more to Sam's aunt's house. I was trying to catch his cousin before he left for work at four o'clock in the morning. I had to pass many traffic lights and streets to get to Sam's aunt's house but by the grace of GOD I made it. Here it was about three or four o'clock in the morning and I remember knocking the door, standing crying, my nightgown half ripped, off bruises everywhere, and eye complete black. I was a nervous wreck, when his cousin came to the door. The first question he asked was, what happen to you? I told him Sam had beat me up, and they were upset. I asked his cousin to take me to the hospital as soon as he could.

After going to the hospital, I was immediately admitted and they keep me. The doctor stated that a human bite is much worse than a dog bite and if I had not made it to the hospital in time I probably would have had to have my entire eye removed. The doctors had me hooked up to IVs and monitored me for a few days. Of course Sam came to visit me later that day. He stood by the bedside crying and told me he was sorry. He had gotten really drunk and had tried some type of acid (drug) with his so call friends. That was the excuse he gave me for almost killing me and not really remembering anything about that night. One would think after all of that and GOD sparing my life to live through it I would never go back to Sam. Where was I going to go at the age of seventeen and who was going to take me in and take care of me? Yes, after a couple days in the hospital Sam came, picked me up, and we went home together. Of course he promised he would not hit me anymore and said all the things that a woman would want to hear. I heard that he was sorry so many times and that he didn't mean to do it. I knew it was not true. Every time Sam drank he would get angry with me for some reason.

This is what left the scar in my eye that nobody noticed but my babysitter, and even if they did notice it they didn't say anything. I immediately changed the subject because I didn't want to get into how awful my life had been while living in Springfield Illinois. I was wrong thinking that I could move back home and everything would be the same way it was before I ever left. My mother was the only person that actually acted the same as before, everyone else acted so differently toward me. My mother noticed how everyone was treating me, as if I didn't belong, and she could tell that I wasn't happy there. Then I called Sam and told him everyone acted as if they didn't want any part of me and to send me money so I could go back to Springfield. A few days later the money arrived. My mother told my father that Sam had sent me money to go back to Springfield and my father said no. He ripped the money up. My father said I could not go back to be with Sam. After a few days my mom was the only one that really showed any signs of love. She told me that she was going to give me money to go back to my husband. The very next day she ask me to find me a ride to the bus station and my mom put me on the bus. She told me that she was sending me back because she loved me and she could not stand to see me being mistreated by everyone, and my father. She also stated that she knew my father would never treat me right and leave down what I had done by running away from home. I told my mom that my dad was going to be mad at her, and she told me not to worry about it, that she knew how to deal with him. She told me that I was a grown woman and I could make it on my own, all I needed to do was to put GOD first and everything would be okay. That sounded good and simple but at the age of seventeen I didn't really understand what that meant. I recalled that I had not been to church since I ran away from home a few years ago. And even when I was in church, growing up, there were times when I didn't really listen to the preacher or even understand what he was preaching about. We had gone to church all the time because we had to go — not because we wanted to go. Sadly that was the last time I saw my mom before she was killed.

I went back to Sam and of course the fighting eventually started back and my life wasn't getting any better. I tried to be the best that I could be and did what I was supposed to do but I was tired of fighting and could not figure out what had I done to deserve it. Sam would always say that I was fat and no one else would want me. After you hear such a negative statement over and over you really don't know what to think. I knew I didn't have anywhere else to go. I felt like my life was useless. Why was I even here on earth? It seemed as though everywhere I went I was getting mistreated in some way. People always treated me like I was nobody, as though I didn't even exist.

Every month my father continued to send me support until I turned eighteen. I had a real father; he continued to help support me even after running away from home.

I still thought I was in love with Sam. At this point I knew my family no longer wanted a part of me. I felt that although I was in an abusive marriage Sam stilled loved me, besides where was I going to go? People remembered me as the young girl that ran away from home. I am sure everyone thought I would never amount to anything because of the unwise choices that I had made. When you can't go back home and don't feel loved or welcomed, you have to make and create your own home for yourself. Never did it dawn on me that this was real life and this was how it is going to be and nothing would change until I changed it. I was doing the same thing and looking for different results but I was getting the same results. I found myself being sad and disappointed all the time. There were times when I hated being alive. People were making me feel like I didn't even belong on earth. Sam was so abusive and demanding. I was really angry inside and he didn't realize that he was turning me against him. I just didn't have anywhere else to go so that is why I put up with his drama for so long. Drugs and alcohol was a big part of our life and I was tired of being involved in it and Sam was becoming more violet toward me. When he got drunk or high I would always become his target victim, especially if I asked him where had he been. Those were fighting words in our home.

We use to go to card games every weekend and there would always be this older guy there, he was a friend of the family. His name was Nathaniel. One night he finally got a chance to talk to me and he asked me why I never smiled and was always sad all the time. He stood back weekend after weekend and watched Sam jump on me, call me names etc. He stated, "That man does not love you," and I said to him, "How do you know that, you don't know him?" He told me that if Sam really loved me he would not beat on me and treat me like that. He also said that Sam was not aware of what he had. What Nathaniel didn't know, or anyone else, was that I was very angry inside. No matter what I did Sam would not be satisfied and it appeared that whatever he said, it had to be. I never had a say in anything, I mean anything. Sam was the boss, that was also turning me against him. It was Sam's way or no way. I really thought Sam loved me but when Nathaniel told me what he did, it really made sense. I didn't realized that Sam's beating on me like a punching bag meant that he didn't love me. There were other members of Sam' family getting beat up by their spouses or companions as well, and nobody ever left their spouse. Every woman in our circle was being abused and they made it seem as though this was how it was suppose to be. I could not figure that out, but no one ever left, and if they did they always went back. Nathaniel was a much older guy, old enough to be my father if not my grandfather.

Drinking and playing cards on weekends would make me forget about the drama that Sam was capable of. He would go out some nights and come home then take it out on me because things didn't go well with him and his women in the streets. There were also many times when we would end up fighting in public, in clubs, stores, etc., Sam didn't care where we were. I never told my family about the fighting that was going on in my life. I was a victim of domestic violence the entire marriage until I decided to actually end it. This is always a part of life people don't really tell because if you don't see it you don't really know it's going on. I was in Springfield and I didn't have my family there and I never told them anything about my years of abuse. My life has been dramatized for years just because people made it seem as though you didn't have choices — when you really do.

We had been together for almost three years. I graduated from high school and we finally had our first baby, little Sammie Jr. I went seven months of my pregnancy without telling my mom because I wanted to surprise her when the baby was born. But for some reason I kept getting this feeling deep down inside to tell her and I was beginning to feel guilty because I hadn't told her. I told my sister who lived in Chicago, she can't hold water and she ended up telling my mom. I told my mom that I was planning on surprising her once the baby was born. My mother knew that I had always wanted and loved babies and she knew that I was hoping for a girl. The next couple of months my mom waited for the baby to be born. I called her on September 9, 1986 and told her that I had a little boy and we had named him little Sammie Jr. She laughed because she knew I was hoping for a little girl and she knew I was looking forward to little dresses and ponytails. However, I told her that as soon as I got out of the hospital I would be sending her pictures of her grandson.

They kept me in the hospital a bit longer than expected. My mom told me that she was going to send her grandbaby some money.

We got home with the baby and tried to get adjusted. There were no instructions and Sammie Jr. did not sleep at night at all. He cried almost all the time and I had no idea that this much work came with an infant it was overwhelming for me. My mom was almost seven hundred miles away or more, so I knew I would not get the additional help that I needed. My first plan was to keep the baby a secret and just bring the baby to her when the it was born but that was not in GOD's plan. I was so overwhelmed until I called the doctor to see if I could come back to the hospital and put my baby back in the nursery for a few more days. The doctor told me it didn't work like that, I would be fine. He told me to try to get some rest and to keep the baby comfortable and dry. I would talk to mom and tell her how the baby would not sleep at night. She would laugh, and tell me that all comes with it. I also let her knew that I had received the money that she had sent. I told my mom that I had put her pictures of my baby in the mail and she should be getting them real soon.

I had been home with my crying baby day after day when Sam got us tickets to his brother's college basketball game. I decided that I would take a break from my crying baby and go on my first outing. The game was located in Peoria Illinois, not too far from Springfield. It was a Friday evening and my baby was about two weeks old and we decided to leave him with a couple of Sam's family members who weren't going to the game. The entire time I was at the game I could not get into it. For some reason my heart was not at ease. I just thought that it was just me feeling guilty that I had left my newborn baby for the first time. A lot of things were going through my mind because my baby was so small. He was only about two weeks old. But that was not it, even though I didn't say anything to Sam about it, something just did not feel right. I continued to sit through the entire game but my mind was not there. I was trying to figure out why I was feeling like. I was saying to myself that I was ready to go home, that something must have happened. I had the feeling that something awful had happened but I didn't know what it could be. After the games we normally would go to his brother's dorm for awhile to sit and talk about their wins or loses. Most of the family would attend the games as well. Everything always turned out to be a family event and a party with Sam's family. I think this was what I loved so much. The feeling of having a family and feeling accepted was what kept me in his family for so long.

It was getting late and we finally decided to go home. As we were approaching Springfield, Sam and I were wondering if little Sam had kept everyone up, because he only took cat-naps. We pulled up to the house and all the lights in the house were on. It was late at night so you know what was going through our mind. As we walked in the door my aunt-in-law told me to sit down, I immediately thought that something had happen to my baby. When she said sit down I was so afraid of what was next, she said my family had been in a bad car accident and she believed it killed my mom and my sisters. I told her that can't be so because I had just talked to mom. I didn't know what to think, I could not even remember my mom's phone number and I had just talked to her the night before. Sam finally was able to get the number and I talked to my dad and he said he didn't know what really happened but it had been a terrible accident. My mom and two of my sisters had been in the car and they had a head-on collision with a truck. One of my older sisters had been driving and my mom was in the passenger seat. My baby sister was in the backseat and the accident happened about 5:30 p.m. The accident happened during the same time we were driving to Peoria for the basketball game. The accident was directly in front of Ruleville Hospital in Mississippi. The impact was so bad it crushed every bone in my mom's body killing her instantly and my baby sister was thrown out the back window breaking her neck. My sister who had been driving was knocked out and didn't remember a thing. She was flown to a specialist hospital in Jackson Mississippi. At this point I didn't know what to think and how and what I was feeling. My whole life had changed once again in just one night. My life has not been the same since. There I was eighteen years old with a two-week-old baby, in a domestic violent marriage and my mom was gone. What was I going to do? I thought to myself, my life is a mess. I felt totally lost and I felt like I didn't have any choices in life. I felt totally empty inside.

The very next day I went to Mississippi to be with the remainder of my family and when I went to the mail box I found the pictures of my baby that I had sent my mom. She never got to see them because the pictures arrived the day after she was killed. Another disappointment I had to live with. I didn't know what to do, I didn't know what to think, I didn't know what I was feeling and nobody cared about me. My mom had been the only person who always told me that she loved me and she was always the same toward me no matter what. What was I going to do? My heart was hurting and empty for a long time. I thought after going through all of that and losing my mom and baby sister at the same time plus another sister in critical condition in the hospital that Sam would have a heart and do what was right. Sam did not change.

After the double funeral service for my mom and baby sister was over, everything went right back to the way it was. Everyone knew the story and he didn't change, if anything Sam got worse. It was only a few months after that when we got into a heated fight once again and the police were called again. I decided to take my baby and go to a shelter. After sitting at the shelter for a few hours my mind was not at ease. Deep down inside I had the urge to go back home. At about two o'clock in the morning I called a cab to pick us up so we could go back home. Another big surprise—I caught Sam in my bed with another women. Sam had the nerve to say he didn't know who she was. How stupid do men think we are? After that I really didn't want Sam to touch me anymore because I knew I could not trust him.

Our marriage was as good as being over after that. There I was disappointed again and just tired of everything but I had nowhere to go or nobody to turn to. So I decided to pack me and my baby's clothes and leave Sam. I was feed up, tired of all the fighting, and women that I had to cope with, and unnecessary drama. I moved in with a so-called friend. After staying with her for a few days I found out she had been sleeping with Sam as well. My heart was so hurt from everything that had been happening in my life. I really didn't know what to do. I knew I could not trust Sam anymore. When you really don't trust a person it is hard to actually love him. I didn't have anywhere else to go, no friends, no family so what could I do? It felt like the entire world was against me and I didn't have anywhere else to go, so you can guess where I ended up.

I ended up going right back to Sam, back to the abusive marriage because I had nowhere else to go. Every so-called friend that I thought I had, Sam had already been with or tried to be with. At this point I could not trust anyone, especially women. I spent many years running in and out of shelters, sharing my story with all the other battered women and we all ended up going right back to our abusive spouses. Being a victim of domestic violence is no joke. It tends to alter your mind at times, you do what you have to do. In most cases we go back to our abuser because we don't have anywhere else to go. You can only live in a shelter for so long, then where do you go if you don't have anywhere else to go or any type of support system? What do you do? I have heard many people say, "Why would you keep going back to him and he keeps beating you?" When you decide to leave you don't get any help or support from anyone especially the people who have given you the advice to leave, so you don't have a choice but to go back to the abuse. You know you will be taken care of and the bills will get paid. It is called survival—I know it sounds crazy but it is the truth. How do you make it without any help or additional support or any type of support system? I found out and learned that people would not help you in most cases, and if they did there was something they wanted in return. I know it could be done, but it would be such a struggle working making minimum wage and trying to pay daycare cost, rent, etc.

It seemed as though all I was getting in life was a lot of heartaches, pain, and disappointments. Nothing ever went right, no matter what it was. Not once was I ever asked how was I feeling about the loss of my family. Nobody cared about what I was feeling at all. Everything continued to go on like nothing had ever happened and no one showed any type of compassion at all. I had actually lost my mother and baby sister and an older sister was hospitalized in critical condition, did anyone care about that? I went to a double funeral service that really hurt my heart but who cared about that? I was never asked, "How do you feel, are you okay?" I never had a shoulder to cry on. I don't even know what that would feel like. No one would really understand how I felt anyway because everyone in our circle had their parents at the time. I was beginning to see that people really didn't care.

I continued on with my life. I tried to make the best out of my marriage. I realized that mom is gone and she wasn't coming back. However, in the meantime I was focusing on a way to get out of this marriage alive. We were fighting to kill, but nobody ever ended up in the hospital except me. I was at work one day, about a year later, and got another disturbing telephone call. A next-door neighbor had noticed that my father had not left for work and that was very unusual for him. My dad's neighbor broke into the house and found my father in bed in a deep sleep. He immediately called the ambulance and my father was rushed to the hospital. My father had suffered a stroke in his sleep and they kept him on the breathing machine until we all could make it to see him. At this point I knew this was it, this was the last person in my life who really loved me — I was his daughter. I felt like my life was over. I had already seen almost everything that my dad had warned us about while growing up, how people don't really care about you and you don't really have true friends. So I knew that nothing about my life was going to be easy at this point and I was still a teenager. Mom and Dad are the ones that actually kept the family together, now that my mom and dad were gone I knew I wasn't going a have family or anything even close to that ever again, the family together, now that mom and dad is gone the family will all go their separate ways and this will be the end of it. I knew I was more than likely going to be spending the rest of my life the best way I could — alone. True enough this is what happened to my family, now we only see each other at funerals and that is only if they chose to tell me about the death. I have not had the feeling of a family since I left home in 1984. It has been so long, I don't even know what that feels like anymore.

As the years continued to pass I got tired of the fighting with Sam and constantly leaving him and coming back for the same reason. I could never get any type of help to make it on my own. Every time I left it just seemed as though everyone were taking advantage of me, taking my kindness for weakness. Everybody that I tried to stay with would basically just want my money and have the nerve to ask me if I was saving my money for my own place. It was really a dead end situation because I have always had to try and make it by myself. I never had family or anyone to give me an extra helping hand. My son was getting older and watching us fight like cats and dogs. He saw me crying over and over again and hated to see me cry. He was five years old when he said, "Mom why do you keep going back to dad, you know he is just going to keep beating you." I took that as GOD speaking to me, something clicked.

All the years we had been together had been nothing but drama, fight after fight, woman after woman, and there was never a reason. Sam would always tell me nobody else wanted me, that I was fat, ugly and had a baby. Where was I going to go? He would tell me that no one else wanted me because I had a baby. Sam thought that I would never leave him. I got tired, I wasn't happy, nor was I feeling loved at all by Sam anymore. I had not been happy for years. I left Sam many times but I always ended up going back. It seemed like every time I left and tried to stay with someone else I was being taking advantage off in some kind of way. It was like I could not win no matter what and I could never get ahead. People were using me for their benefits not mine, no one really wanted to help me. They just wanted whatever they could get out of me and I was beyond tired of dealing with phony people. After knowing about so many of Sam's women and finding him in bed with one, I really didn't want to be touched by him. I dreaded him touching me. I felt that there was no purpose for it because it meant nothing to me anymore. So from that point on having sex with my husband was like being raped over and over again.

After moving back and forth and in and out of shelters for over ten years of my life I was beyond tired, so I decided I was not going to take it anymore. I was worth more than that and I had better leave him before one of us ended up getting killed. So I left and moved on with my life. I decided to go ahead and file for divorce. I thought at this point everything would be over and Sam would now leave me alone. But I was totally wrong. Life didn't work like that because we shared a child together which meant divorced or not we had to have some type of communication for the rest of our life.

Chapter 3

Life with Maurice

As time went on and I was trying to adjust without Sam being in my life. It was hard because Sam took me out of my parents home and this meant I was used to someone supporting me. Now that Sam and I had gone our separate ways I was on my own with no other type of support from anyone and it was hard. It was a struggle because I never knew that men really didn't give you any money to help support their child unless you go to court to get an order from the judge. This was new to me as well. I never knew that some men didn't take care of their kids unless they were actually with you. I thought most men were like my father but I was dead wrong. Sam would get his son almost weekend but when it came to money or school clothes he would not give me a dime and if he bought him any clothes he would keep them at his house. I had never heard of anything like that in my life. Therefore I had to try to take care of everything on my own and it was not easy at all. I had to do all the picking up and dropping off all by myself.

Sam's family would no longer keep little Sam for me but they would keep little Sam for Sam if he needed them to. I never understood that either. When you divorce I didn't know that you were divorcing the whole family, I'd never heard of such a thing. As long as I was in the marriage the family would call me names like crazy and stupid for letting Sam do the things that he did to me, but when I divorced Sam his family acted as if they no longer knew me. This didn't make my life any easier. I really didn't know anyone in Springfield. His family I knew I didn't have any friends but I was not expecting them to act the way they did toward me. I never did anything to anyone to get the type of treatment that I was getting from his family. I spent many years of my life being a baby-sitter for his family and a baby-sitter was something that I could never get for my child for some reason. When they did see me they would look at me like they didn't even know who I was or like I had done something to them, but what they didn't know was I was running for my own life. I wasn't in a position to wonder why people were acting the way that they were acting or treating me because no one was helping me. So it really didn't matter what people were thinking about me. This was just a turning point in my life, I was realizing that people only want you around for their benefit and could care less about anyone besides themselves. I was still young and learning so I could not be mad at anyone, I just knew that I had not mistreated anyone or did them wrong in any way so I had to get over it and move on with my life. One thing about people is the truth about them will eventually come out and when it does you have to believe what they show you. Most people are not real and in most cases it is just a front and there is normally a motive behind people pretending that they like you or are being nice to you.

Then I met Maurice, a guy at work. He appeared to be nice, kept insisting on dating me, and telling me that I should move on with my life. "Oh give yourself a chance," he would tell me. All the time I was afraid to date someone else because Sam would always tell me that if he could not have me no one else could. Maurice kept telling me that everyone was not the same. He already knew some of the bad things that I had gone through with my ex-husband because he worked with me and he knew that my ex-husband was not allowed on my job at all, this was an order from the police. I kept restraining orders on Sam until I left Springfield, just to be on the safe side. I figured it was best to try to be safe than sorry. Maurice also felt that I was somewhat afraid of Sam and was trying to keep my distance from Sam as much as possible. I always knew that Sam would use his son to come by whenever he felt like it. This is the reason I was hiding out from him. So I would hide out with Maurice after work so Sam would not find me. Although we were no longer together, I still had in the back of my mind that anything could happen. Sam would come by my place unexpected saying he wanted to see his son. I knew deep down in my heart that as long as I was living in Springfield Sam was not going to let me have a successful relationship or marriage with anyone else. It appeared that Sam's goal was to just keep me for himself and treat me any way he wanted to and have as many women as he wanted too. He didn't want to give someone else a chance to treat me right. Sam was a nice person and always provided for me but drugs and alcohol was a major part of his life that he didn't know how to handle. The drugs and alcohol just made him more violent than ever because he could not hold his liquor. If Sam was drinking, he was going to argue with somebody. I was always the main victim for some reason.

Maurice would be nice to me like he really cared. At the time I was afraid so I felt that I would be protected. I wasn't ready to date anyone because I knew I stilled had feeling for Sam even after all the things I'd gone through with him. I was just trying to move on so I could forget about Sam but it didn't work out that way. Maurice kept being nice to me and my son. After a while Sam heard that I was dating someone else. Sam was not pleased with this at all, he told me he didn't want another man trying to raise his son and that I was always going to be his wife no matter what. Little Sammie was crazy about his daddy. Every weekend he would sit and wait for Sam to pick him up and if he wasn't coming Little Sammie would get disappointed and wanted to know why he wasn't coming. Little Sammie never let anyone try and take the place of his daddy. Running scared from Sam I ended up just falling in the first man arms that came along—a huge mistake. I knew I still had feelings for Sam—the only man I had ever been with. I really didn't know anything different.

Being in an abusive relationship for all those years really had an effect on me and I wasn't thinking. All the broken heartaches that I had endured for the last few years of my life were still there and none of the wounds had healed at all. But I never had anyone to talk to that I could trust or someone in my corner to give me any good advice. I was just continually making unwise choices with my life and not realizing that things were not right until it was almost too late. Everything happened so fast and I had grown up too fast with not many positive situations around me to build on. I wasn't aware that I was falling into the same type of relationship all over again — the drugs, alcohol, gambling etc. Of course when drugs and alcohol are involved no one is sober enough to think right and it's never love it is just the lust of the flesh.

After running and hiding out with Maurice for a period of time and we decided to be in a committed relationship. It seemed like everything was happening very fast. Maurice and I would go to St. Louis almost every weekend to gamble, etc. and visit his family. I would be with Maurice every day after work because we were working together and the next thing I knew was I pregnant. Maurice seemed as though he was so happy and glad that I was pregnant. He stated that he wanted a family and wanted to raise his child. After I found out that I was pregnant, I was sober and realized that I didn't want to be with Maurice for the rest of my life. Everything was done under the influence without thinking things through. I could not stand it when Maurice touched me anymore so I knew at this point we were not going to stay together. Maurice was really being nice to me but I didn't really love him. He waited on me hand and foot while I was pregnant but I just didn't want to be with him. He would tell me all the time that he loved me and I better not ever leave him.

Sam was still trying to intrude in my life. He didn't care for Maurice and he would not let us live in peace. Throughout my whole pregnancy Sam would always have some type of drama when he came to get his son. Sam was not taking this well at all. I was pregnant and he still considered me to be his wife. I didn't get pregnant to hurt Sam, everything happened so fast and nothing was ever thought through or planned correctly.

After I got pregnant, I was sick because I knew I was pregnant by a man that I didn't want to spend the rest of my life with. I was devastated all over again. I spent my entire pregnancy sad and depressed and weighed in at 300 pounds at the time of delivery. This was the point in my life when I knew I needed to make a change, nothing was going right and I needed positive directions and influences. A friend of the family, Nathaniel, had already told me about GOD, so at this point I needed and wanted to try GOD for myself. I was tired of making all these unwise choices and I knew the consequences I was going to have to live and deal with for the rest of my life. My soul was beyond tired. Now I had two children from two different relationships and I really didn't want to be with either one of the fathers. I had gotten so huge I had to wear my maturity clothes almost three to four months after the baby was born. Somebody made a comment to me and said, "How on earth did you let yourself get so big?" After that comment I knew I have to do something. I felt terrible inside and out when she said that and I was not happy with myself at all. This was when I realized that if I didn't even love myself, how could I love someone else and the issues that come along with them. So in 1992 I decided to commit my life back to Christ. I was tired of getting disappointed over and over again and just letting people take advantage of me.

By January of 1993 I had dropped over 100 pounds and I tried my best to make things work with Maurice but I knew I did not love him and didn't want him to touch me. I would find myself getting high everyday just trying to cope and forget about things. Maurice would always tell me how he loved me so much and I better not ever leave him or he would hurt me but I was not feeling that way toward him at all. I knew that I had to tell Maurice that I didn't love him, I didn't want to live a lie pretending that I loved him when I didn't. I just didn't know how or when to tell him, Maurice was a nice person but he was not for me. I still didn't even know what love was and didn't know how to love myself so I knew I would be no justice for him at all. Even after trying to make the best of our relationship for as long as I could I could not take living that lie knowing that I did not love him. I would not let him touch me so I knew it wasn't going to last too long anyway.

I finally found and built the nerve to tell Maurice that I didn't want us to be together and he stated, "If you don't love me then give me back my ring." I took of his ring and gave it back to him and the very next day when I got home from work Maurice had cleared the house out and abandoned his daughter. Maurice would never be able to understand why I did what I did. He really didn't have a clue of what my life was like before he met me. I was really hurting at the time I met Maurice but I did know that I didn't want to be in a relationship. I told him but he would not take no for an answer. Men hear what we say but they don't listen and understand what we mean. I was still trying to cope with life as it was and trying to figure out how to change my own life. I had to do it because I was not even emotionally prepared to be in another relationship—it would not have been fair to neither one of us to continue in this relationship. So I had to tell him that I didn't love him and we had rushed into things too fast. His daughter Kathryn was about two years old and he erased both of us from of his life. He didn't want anything else to do with me or her because I chose to be honest and not lie or pretend that I loved him. He said he was punishing me for this, he was not an active dependable father in his daughter's life until she was fifteen and a half years old. From the age of two through fifteen and a half he probably kept her maybe three times. I remember this so well because we struggled all those years. He didn't do what he was supposed to do and hard times are not easily forgotten by anyone. You could almost count the times he actually saw or kept her on one hand. I can't even begin to tell you how my daughter's life was affected by not having a consistent father in her life. She never received birthday money, cards, calls, Christmas gifts etc. or anything else from her father. Every so often he would call and wish her a happy birthday, if he remembered, or when he wanted to.

My daughter took all those frustrations, of her father not being in her life, out on me, making my life a living hell. I was always trying to figure out why I was getting punished. I was doing everything I could for her but she didn't appreciate it. She always stated that she wanted her father, but her father could not understand that concept. For some reason he thought that because he was paying seventy-four dollars every two weeks for child support he was actually doing his part as a father. For many years, ever since Kathyrn started going to school, I have had to sit in the back of the classroom on several occasions because of her behavior problems. This was more than a challenge for me and no one ever knew what I had to deal while raising Kathryn all by myself. She was acting out because her father wanted no part of her in his life. The only break that I would get from Kathyrn would be the three times her father actually picked her up when we lived here in Chicago. This was from January 1997 until 2007—very long years.

I was basically a single parent from the time Kathyrn was two years old and it was not easy, by no means. Her father never understood the challenges of taking care of a child and not having additional support for necessary things in life. I was not be able to relate to how she was feeling because I had both my parents in my life. I decided to run away from home but both parents were always there for me. When her father and I went our separate ways our daughter was too young to even remember her father. He made no attempts to continue in her life as a father. Was I supposed to live a lie and stay with him or follow my heart? I followed my heart that was true because I had a sober mind the entire time that I was pregnant and had time to think about what I had done without thinking clearly. I knew I had to deal with the consequences of raising my children by myself but I just could not take staying in another abusive relationships anymore whether it was physical or mental. I could not do it so I chose not to do it. I didn't feel loved in abusive relationships and mental abuse was just as bad. A man is quick to say, "I won't hit or beat you," but mental abuse rips at your heart and mind.

Now I had two children and was working a fulltime job at a fast food restaurant. I did not qualify for a better paying job because I did not have the opportunity to go to college. Times were really hard trying. I had to get Kathyrn to daycare and make sure Lil Sammie got to school every day. Neither father would give me cash money nor were they available to drop off their kid at the daycare or school. I always had that job no matter what. It was really hard trying to survive on my salary and the little bit of child support that Sam was paying for his son. Maurice would not give me a dime and would not even take Kathryn on weekends. I would be totally exhausted at times. Sam decided to take Kathyrn on the weekends when he picked up his son. I really appreciated it because that was the only way I got a moment for myself. I'd think about what I needed to do to better my life for me and my kids because this was not working out at all.

Finally in 1995, after waiting almost two years, Maurice's child support came through, seventy-four dollars every two weeks. It was almost impossible to take care my home, car, daycare etc. and two kids on my salary and the small amount of child support that

I was getting for them. I was never able to do anything for my kids but I tried to keep a roof over our heads. It doesn't matter where one lives, it is hard to survive on one small income and take care of two kids. I was working at the fast food restaurant as a crew manager and I had to open the store every morning, which meant I had to be at work at 4:00 am every morning, Monday through Friday. I had to have my kids up by 1:30 am and dressed and dropped off at the sitter by 3:00 am. In order to find a sitter that would actually work those hours I had to take my chances and just go through the yellows pages. There was only one sitter that would take my kids at that time of the morning and she was a Caucasian. It didn't matter because I didn't have anyone else in the city of Springfield that would keep my kids. I had to do what I had to do to survive.

In 1996 I went to work and turned my keys in. After working for the same fast food company almost ten years, I was tired and ready to go. I told my boss that I was finished, that I needed to make a change I was tired of going around in circles and not being able to support my kids. I started beauty school and completed it within 10 months. I lived in my home for one year, not paying the mortgage, but just living off my equity while I completed beauty school. I have never experienced the opportunity of sitting down at a Thanksgiving dinner with me and my kids, or just going shopping, buying school clothes, buying birthday gifts, Christmas gifts etc. I didn't know what that felt like, doing those things for my kids. I have never been in a position to do this for my kids.

I was so tired of struggling in Springfield, Illinois, I called my sister in Chicago and began to open up and tell her about the struggles and the abusiveness that I had gone through plus that I needed to sell my home because it was impossible to live on the little bit that I was getting. I figured if I moved to Chicago things would be different because in Springfield I didn't have any family at all or any type of support system. At this point I was beyond tired because I would always get in a bind and could not even go to the church for help. Although I was a faithful member, paid my tithes and offerings just like any other member did, I found out that the church could only help special people and of course I didn't count. No one has ever considered me as a candidate for being a special person. I always thought that I could go to my own church if nowhere else, but I found out life does not work like that.

My sister told me that I could bring my two kids and live with her until I got a job and got on my feet. This really sounded good because I had many family members and siblings in Chicago. I felt that things would be better because I always thought that family would help each other in the time of need. My kids and I really had hard times while trying to make it in Springfield. Not very many people really knew that and the ones that did, didn't try and help us in any way. They would just try to take what little bit I did have by accepting things from me. They knew I was going to be moving and told me that they would pay me later, but later never came. My kids and I always had to do without but I always did the best I could for my kids with whatever I had because it was not their fault that their fathers and I could not make it together nor was it my fault that they didn't want to help support them financially. Everyone can make it but sometimes we need just a little help along the way. If I had not gone back to church in 1992 and committed my life back to Christ I am sure I would not be here telling my story. Life was getting the best of me and I did not have any positive influences or support system to let me know that I could make it. Drugs and alcohol can easily get the best of you if you allow them too. I had gotten used to that band-aid, drugs and alcohol to make things feel better but only for a moment. I was ready to leave Springfield, I figured that things would not be as bad as the struggle was here in Springfield, trying to raise my kids as a single parent with no help at all. I also knew by moving to Chicago that if the fathers wanted to see their kids they would have to take the drive and pick them up.

In January 1997 I relocated to Chicago, Illinois to make a better life for me and my kids. I sold my home in Springfield and put everything I wanted in storage. I felt that I no longer had a reason to stay in Springfield, there was too much drama and I was struggling all by myself, trying to make it on my own with two children. So I was eager to leave Springfield and begin a new life.

32

Chapter 4

Life Homeless

In January 1997 when we moved to Chicago Kathyrn was just turning five years old and my Lil Sammie was about twelve. When I first arrived to Chicago to live with my oldest sister and her two kids I felt somewhat relieved. I figured we could just help each other. I always thought that was what sisters did. I never knew the cost of living in Chicago was twice the cost of living in Springfield. This meant survival was almost unreal without a good job. As soon as I got to Chicago I enrolled my kids into school, found a church home. I knew I needed to continue my life on the right track and the only way I knew how was to stay in church and continue to trust in GOD. I also found a job fast.

Everything seemed so good at first. I was working as a beautician far out in the suburban area, taking both my kids and my sister two kids to school every day, taking my sister to work every morning and also picking them up. I was driving over a hundred miles a day trying to get everyone to their destination. I could not be late picking up anyone or it would have been a problem, I had to be on time. This was overwhelming for me although my sister would watch Lil Sam while I worked in the evening but she would not watch Kathyrn. I had to pay my uncle to pick Kathyrn up from school and I had to pay my aunt to watch her until I got off work at night. After getting off work at nine or ten o'clock at night I would have to drive to my aunt's house to pick up Kathyrn before I went home. I was exhausted and wasn't making enough money to do anything but pay to get Kathyrn back and forth and try to keep gas in the car. I had to pay my storage bill in Springfield every month because the plan was for me to get my own place. This meant I didn't have any money for anything else. I could tell that this was not going to work out well because I wasn't in a position to save money. All my little money went right back out of my hands plus I was beginning to fill like a taxi driver.

One morning I walked outside and my car was gone, I called the police to report that my car had been stolen. The police came, made a few telephone calls and told me that my car was not stolen — my car had been repossessed. At that point everything changed overnight. I had to find a job closer and learn how to catch the bus to get back and forth. I went to the mall and got a beautician job that same day but the job was commission only. Which meant if I didn't get clients, I didn't get paid. I was working with women that, most of the time, made sure I didn't get any walk-ins. I began inquiring about going to college because I knew there was no way I would be able to survive here in Chicago as a beautician. There were days when I didn't even have bus fare but thank GOD the bus driver understood and would let me ride for free. Some days I would start out walking and get tired and pray that the bus driver would let me ride because the mall was quite a distance from where we lived. I had to take Kathyrn to work with me every Saturday because there was no one in the city of Chicago that would watch her while I went to work.

Things really changed at my sister's house and I didn't feel welcome anymore. Within six months I was homeless. Since I was already used to living in and out of shelters in Springfield I went to the yellow pages and found a shelter that would take me and my kids in. My son didn't want to go to the shelter, he wanted to go back to Springfield to live with his father. My son asked why should he stay in a shelter when he could stay with his dad. Now me and my two kids, the closest thing to a family, had to separate. I made arrangements for Sam to get his son. I told my son that in about a year he could come back to live with me, once I was financially stable and situated in my own place.

I finally located a shelter that would take my daughter and me. The shelter that had an opening was a drug recovery shelter and I accepted it. I put our clothes in a garbage bag and called a cab to pick us up. After we made it to the shelter while I was waiting to get checked in my five year old daughter saw me sitting there crying and she said, "Don't cry mom it won't be like this always." I knew that was GOD again letting me know that everything would be okay. I didn't have a dime to my name after I paid the cab driver and there was no one that I could get a dime from. After getting checked in and situated my daughter and I had to share a room with a total of twenty people, which included about four mothers and their children. I already knew the routine of living in a shelter so it was not anything new for me. I did what I needed to do during my stay.

I decided to call Kathryn's father to see if he could take his daughter for a while because we were living in a shelter. Maurice had not really done anything for her. After we separated it was like he abandoned us so I was hesitant about calling him, but I needed help and she was his daughter. I figured I couldn't get help from anyone else. I should be able to get help from her father because I didn't make her by myself so why should I have to struggle with her all by myself. He pretended to be concerned and said he didn't want his baby living in a shelter so he came and got her for a while.

The shelter had many contacts of other homes available for the homeless, as long as we had goals set for ourselves. I already knew I had to start going to college because working as a beautician was not going to support my daughter and me. After a few weeks I had an interview to get into a shared living home. The interview went well I was able to move from the shelter into the shared living quarters. I had my own room and everybody's room had a lock and key to it. My daughter's father had came and picked her up and took her back to Springfield. My focus now was getting into college while working the job that I had. I wanted to go to school to be a mortician so I took this as my opportunity to do so. By the end of 1997, I found a college where I could study to become a mortician. I got my repossessed car back after six months of waiting.

I enrolled in my classes for the spring of 1998. I went to school Monday through Thursday and worked on Friday and Saturdays. On Sundays I would go to church, which had been a part of my life since I committed my life back to Christ in 1992. I had to keep Christ in my life in order to stay on the right track and in my right mind. When school started I felt really good, that I was actually attending college. There were many times when I wanted to go to college had not been able to do so. I was going to school every day and no one at college knew that I was living in a shelter.

Some of the women in the shelter were really very nice and bought me some of my school supplies for college. Their kindness felt really good and at times I would sit in my room and cry because no one had ever done anything nice like that for me before. Small things really touch the heart. I don't understand why people think big things are important because the small things are what we remember the most. The simple things, for example, just having someone say you can make it, means a lot. The women at both shelters that I stayed in couldn't understand how a person as nice as me could end up in a shelter. I told them I was there for the same reason they were, I didn't have anywhere else to go. Everyone would ask if I had family and I would tell them that they had family as well but that we were all at the shelter, together, for some reason. No one could understand my being there because I had so many siblings and relatives in Chicago. They asked where was my family in times like this? I could not answer or explain that because I didn't even know. My family didn't have a clue that I had lived in a shelter for almost a year and they don't even know where I currently lived. I didn't have a family but I know I was born into a family.

After a few months Maurice realized how much work a child was and he decided to bring her back. I guess he couldn't take it anymore. For him getting up every morning, making sure she got to daycare or school, was not an easy job at all, so he brought her back to me.

I had been living in the shelter for almost a year when my caseworker told me a studio apartment was available if I wanted it. I was really excited and I said of course I wanted it. I took the apartment and didn't have anything in it. My daughter and I would sleep on the floor with nothing but a blanket, but that was okay because the apartment was mine and my goal is to always keep my own place at all cost. I would take my daughter to her school every day before I went to school and take her to work with me on Saturdays. My boss said it would be okay to bring her so I did. Things were really looking up for me. I made arrangements to go to Springfield to get some of my items out of storage (so I would have something in my place) and to visit my son. I was not able to visit my son on a regular bases because I never had the additional money to do so. Because I did not having any family or friends in Springfield Illinois I would have to either drive down and back in one day or have enough money to get a hotel room and stay overnight. Getting a hotel room was not always in my budget so I had to drive down when I could and stay for the day and drive back.

I took classes all of 1998 to get accepted into the Mortuary Science program. I applied for the Mortuary Science Program and was accepted into the program in 1999. I was extremely excited because I was under the assumption that once I completed the mortuary science program that I would be making sufficient money and for once I would be able to support both my kids and be able to buy them more than food.

While going to college and taking my classes to become a Mortician I met a guy name Erick. I had taken a couple of classes with him while taking my prerequisite classes for the program. We went on one dinner date and he told me that GOD said I was going to be his wife. I know I had been praying for GOD to send me a husband because nothing had been right in my other two relationships. I was at the point in my life where I felt that GOD had answered my prayers and sent me the husband to spend the rest of my life with. I told my pastor at the time that I wanted him to meet my fiancé. I thought that he was going to set up us with marriage counseling classes etc. Although he set up an appointment to meet with the both of us, the appointment only lasted about ten minutes or less and he told me this is a fine young man. He actually gave me the okay to marry him and that is exactly what happened.

I was looking for marriage counseling, any type of wisdom or advice that your minster would give before making such a big step, but I didn't get any of that. I really wasn't surprised because this was the same church where I had walked down the aisle and joined, then told the whole congregation that I was homeless and, I kid you not, not a single soul in the church gave me any leads for additional help. It was like I never even existed to this church. I was a faithful member and attended bible classes every week and no matter how much money I made at my job I did what the bible said, gave ten percent and offering. The whole time I was at this particular church I was crying out for help and no one ever heard a word. There were many times when my tithe was only a dollar. I would get a money order and put it in the collection plate but no one ever asked, "Why is this lady making out money orders for one dollar and sometimes even ninety cents etc.?" (which was ten percent of whatever I had made for the entire week).

I felt nobody really cared, that if you didn't have money you really didn't count, but GOD sees and hears everything. That is what kept me going and holding my head up. I know GOD sees and hears everything and I knew deep down inside that my life would not always be the way that it was. I knew that GOD was with me because it appeared that everyone else was against me – I never could count on anyone. I know someday we'll all have to stand before GOD and answer for what we have done, all of us. I wasn't surprised about church folks because in Springfield GOD taught me how things were done. Anytime you go to your church and tell them you are a single mom with two small children and your lights are off, they just tell you that they will pray for you. This told me a whole mouth full, so nothing could surprise me about church folks any more.

Although I had been praying for GOD to send me a husband I thought I was going about things the correct way, by going to my pastor. My pastor gave me the okay and said he was a good guy. I thought this was it so within six weeks we planned the entire church wedding and reception and got married on July 4, 1999. I didn't know at the time that I was jumping into another bear trap again. The only difference between my new husband and the other two was that Erik was in church and the other two hadn't been.

Chapter 5

Life with Erick

After we got married we continued to go to school. As usual everything started out really good. We both were in church, singing in the choir together and going to bible class every week on a regular basis. We did everything as a family. Shortly after we got married, I took Erick to Springfield to meet my son who was still living with his father. When my son met Erik, I could tell that my son was disappointed so when Erick left the room I asked my son what was wrong and he said, "Mom why did you marry this guy? I don't like him and the marriage will never last." At this point I was trying to see how my son determined that so fast.

The first year of my marriage was almost too good to be true but before we made it to our first wedding anniversary Erick had relapsed and was back to using crack cocaine. I came home from school and Erick was not there, it was not like him to not come straight home. As hours passed I begin to get worried so I called the police to put in for a missing person. The police arrived at my house and asked numerous questions about his where abouts and friends etc. I told the police that we were a very close family, we did everything as a family, so I didn't know what could have happened to him. However, the police wanted a little background on Erick. They were asking if he drank alcohol or did drugs. When I told them that he had been clean from crack cocaine for three to four years they both laughed at me and stated, "Your husband has relapsed. You can get out of this marriage right now or you can continue to go through things like this for the next ten to twenty years of your life." Sure enough the next morning Erick came home and his first words were, "I relapsed." All I could say was "Oh my

GOD, Oh my GOD," I knew this was not going to be good but I didn't know the exact extremes of a crack cocaine user. I had to educate myself as quick as possible because I didn't have a clue what my life was going to be like and I knew it had to be a bad situation in order for the policeman to give me the advice to get out now or I would regret it. It was not quite our first wedding anniversary and I didn't just want to put my husband out. I chose to stick by my husband. I was aware of the vows that I had made, it wasn't like this was my first marriage. I knew what the vows meant and I also knew that his addiction to drugs was a sickness. My GOD, what a journey this man took me on.

We lived in a pipe dream for the next five years, it was unreal. I lived in a nightmare and that was no joke at all. We both continued to go to school and of course he thought he was hiding his drug problem. We both graduated at the same time with our degrees. I completed school to become a mortician but I was not going to go to work right away because I didn't want to enable Erick's drug habit, so I continued to go to school. I knew I wanted to further my education and this gave me a good opportunity to do it. Erick was making more than enough to support us so I didn't want to jump into making additional money to support his drug addiction, which he blamed on me. After continuing to go to school for about another year, it began to be a problem for Erick. He was not pleased with me because I was still going to school so to keep the peace in the home I decided to put my schooling on hold and start my apprenticeship as a mortician. Erick was in and out of rehab centers, was getting jobs and was not keeping them long. He argued about money, played mind games with me and lied all the time. I used to have to run to the bank every payday to withdraw his check before he got to it. I was so exhausted in this marriage. My previous relationships seemed great compared to the mental abuse this man put me through.

When Erick started back using drugs in 2000 our marriage at that point was over. All he wanted was the drug. His body would be home but his mind was far away from being with me. For the third time I entered into a committed relationship, one where I no longer wanted him to touch me anymore and couldn't trust him at all. We never had an intimate relationship from the very beginning for some reason. He would leave and be gone anywhere from two to three weeks at a time and then come back home and act as if nothing had ever happened. I stayed with Erik and tried to do whatever a wife was supposed to do. I wasn't new to marriage, I understood my vows, and I knew my husband was sick. I tried over and over and over to help him as much as I could but I realized that I could not help someone who did not want to be helped. It was useless and no one else was getting tired and stressed out, just me.

After putting my schooling on hold in the fall of 2002 I decided to go to work to do my apprenticeship as a mortician. I started working and making eight dollars an hour. I loved my job. While doing my apprenticeship a funeral director really helped me to cope with what I was going through at home. What a great feeling I had at the end of the day after I'd helped a family plan their loved ones funeral arrangements. Every opportunity I got I would sit in on the funerals just to hear a word from GOD. I loved my job. It was giving me the strength to hold on and keep the faith and it was helping me build my own personal relationship with GOD. At work no one ever knew why I always wanted to sit in on every funeral service. I truly miss being a funeral director. Sometimes I just feel empty inside because I have a passion for that, I never considered it a job, it was more of a ministry, and I miss it. I have to assume that GOD has something else for me to do. This just brought joy to my soul, GOD put us here on earth to help one another not hurt each other. I would get such a great pleasure out of helping people on my job because that was what GOD wanted me to do. Treat people the way you want to be treated and always try to help someone. I never understood how many people don't realize that this is what GOD wants us to do. That is why we are here on earth together. Don't do to people what you don't want done to you. I would look forward to going to work. I really did love my job. It gave me strength and motivation to keep my head up and be strong.

Erick didn't change, he would still use drugs, he would only stay clean long enough to get another job and everything would start all over again. GOD knew at that point in my life my soul was tired. I would sit up at night and just cry out to GOD because things were unreal and way out of my control. I knew that only GOD could handle this one. I was aware that GOD was not going to allow anything to happen to me that I could not deal with, and each situation would give me the courage and strength to go on. The things that I had to go through with Erick. If I hadn't known GOD I would have taken my own life. Erick always tried to blame me for his relapses because he didn't want to quit using drugs. He was stressing me out so badly. I never knew when he was coming home or what he was up to. There would be times when I would come home from work and the house would be unlocked because he was in such a hurry to get out the door when I left. There were also times when he didn't have his key and he would climb through the window to get in, it was awful. I knew this was not going to go on forever but it really did seem like it.

We actually stayed married for five years and the things that I went through made it seem like the longest five years of my life. I got up one morning and looked in the mirror and could hardly recognize myself, I knew this marriage was getting the best of me. I had to step back and let GOD be GOD. This situation was too big for me and I was aware of it. Erick would be just coming in, high on crack cocaine, and would drive us to bible class like nothing happened. He loved to argue about anything, it didn't matter what it was it could have been something as simple as cookies. If the box said twenty-four cookies and there were only twenty-three cookies he would take it out on my daughter. I would swear that we didn't take one but he was convinced that the box was always right. This would end up being a thirty-minute argument or more. We dealt with this type of mental abuse for five long, long, years. I was so exhausted in this marriage but I didn't know what to do. It was now 2003 and nothing had changed. I just loved my job. Although I was still just making eight dollars an hour I'd get up every morning, thank GOD, and was prepared to do my ministry at work.

One morning Erick got up, got dressed, went to work, and I have not seen or heard from his since. I waited six months to hear something from him, and I never did. Then I packed up all of his clothes and made arrangements for his family to get them. I was able to get a divorce in thirty days because he abandoned my daughter and I.

I prayed to GOD to not let us cross each other's path ever again. It has been six years now and GOD has granted me that request. This was the end of my relationship with Erick. The financial mess he left for me took a couple of years or more to clean up. I had to learn how to survive here in Chicago off of eight dollars an hour.

Erick left during one (out of all the years that we have been here) of the two summers that Kathyrn was with her father. When she made it back I told her Erick had left me. She said, "Thank GOD and I don't want another stepdad, I don't know why you married him anyway I could have told you it wasn't going to work, but who'd listen to me, I was a seven year old kid." She also said, "Mom how could you not see the signs, there was always something about him that I didn't like but I really could not pin-point it."

Erick had really messed up our finances. I was making eight dollars an hour, and shortly after he left I ended up getting my wages garnished because of something that he'd done. I was devastated! I was trying to take care of my living expense and my daughter and was now making less than eight dollars an hour. I went to public aid for help and they told me I was making too much to qualify for help and they couldn't help it that my wages were being garnished. Believe me when I say this was unreal. Only GOD knows how we made it from 2003 to 2005. Erick knew he had messed things up so badly and he had the nerve to walk away and not look back. I am ok with this because I believe what goes around does come back around. After Erick left in 2003 it took time for me to decide what I should do next. The only way I was able to live through this tragedy was by staying with GOD the entire time.

By the end of 2004 I had made up in my mind that I wanted, and needed, to get back into college and continue where I left off in 2002. I enrolled in classes at the end of 2004 and in January of 2005 when I began college I made up in my mind that I wasn't going to stop until I get the highest degree to be earned. I knew it was going to be a struggle but for me anything worth having does not come easy. I am still paying today for twenty years of relationships that came so easy in my life. So I was ready and willing to make the sacrifice and go back to school. I didn't have anything to lose.

There was never money for anything and Kathyrn's father was still paying me for child support, the exact same seventy-four dollars every two weeks that was ordered back in 1995. He never gave any extra and sometimes didn't even pay that. I know I had to lean on GOD because there was no one in my corner but GOD. I had to drop off and pick up my daughter every day. I had to plan my life, job, etc., around her. There was never anyone around to help me out so I did what I needed to do. I would ask for raises at work but it was never enough to make ends meet. Nobody had a clue how my daughter and I were living. I would have to leave work every day to pick her up from school and my boss had a problem with that but what was I suppose to do. If I didn't pick her up who was going to get her. I didn't care how my boss felt about it. He didn't know my story nor did he care anyway. Even if someone could have picked her up for me how was I going to pay for that expense? We could not even eat off of the salary that I was making. I knew it was time to actually show my daughter how GOD was working in our lives and how GOD was looking out for us because nobody else was.

I was not making anywhere near enough to take care of our living expenses with my low paying job. I was trying to pay rent, car payment, utilities, etc. I was working fulltime, going to school, doing what I was supposed to do, but there was no way I could continue to work five or six days a week and still not make enough to eat. On Monday nights my daughter and I would go to a small chicken place on Seventy-first and Jeffery. I would take her in with me, tell her to sit down, and I would walk up to the counter and ask whoever was working, "Could you please give me food for two of us? It doesn't matter if it is cold or old, we just need food to eat." They never questioned me at all and we would go almost every Monday. It was the only way to actually get meat to eat. I would try to give them the little change that I had but they would not take it. No matter how many Mondays we went they gave us food and I was never questioned, I knew this was GOD working in our lives. We would go to pantries, and churches, wherever we had to do to get food. Most places didn't give out meat for some reason. There were times when I would drive up to the gas station and tell the cashier I needed gas to get to work but I didn't have any money and the cashier would allow me to get gas. My daughter was thrilled, she saw GOD working in our lives. On Wednesday night bible class my daughter would help one of the ladies at the church, passing out the outlines for the night and she would give her two dollars. This would help us get something to eat and if she didn't give it to her we didn't eat. My daughter didn't understand why no one would help us. There were people that knew our situation but would not offer us anything because we never looked needy to them. She would always question me and ask, "Mom where is your family? I never heard of anything like that, where are they?" She did not realize that my family really didn't want anything to do with me. I always assumed it was because of how I left home when I was a young teenager.

I have been without my family ever since I was fifteen or sixteen years old so at this point in my life I feel that I don't have a family. No relatives have been active in my life since my parents died and that has been over twenty years. My daughter really doesn't know anyone in my family besides the sister that we lived with for six months. I wanted them to get to know each other but my sister never wanted to be bothered, so what was I suppose to do. My daughter always wanted to see if she could spend a night and my sister would always ask, "What does your mom have to do?" My daughter could tell that my sister didn't want to be bothered. She started making excuses as to why Kathyrn could not spend a night. So I told my daughter to stop bothering her. I never really knew why my family was the way they were, I just assumed that everyone was different and wanted to live their own separate lives.

I had been through so much and I know when people don't want to be bothered so I just leave them alone. My daughter would ask me, "If you died mom what would happen to me?" I could never answer that question. She only knew me, she really didn't know anyone else, and she wanted her father in her life. I taught my daughter how to survive if something happened to me, I taught her how to do everything, and I taught her how to recognize GOD. I spent all those years teaching her to treat people the way she wanted to be treated and to always try to give to people that were less fortunate. My daughter had been born and raised in the church, and I tried to teach her, as best as I could, how important

45

it was to do what was right because GOD will always supply our needs. There were times when I went to different churches for food and the doors were closed in my face because I was not a member there. There were times when I would go into the grocery store and tell the manager that I needed food for my daughter and me, he would give me a basket and let me pick out some items. My daughter would ask her father for some money but he would tell her he had too many bills to pay and would ask her what was I doing with the child support money he gave us. There were times when our gas was off in our home. We did what we had to do, and as far as shopping, that was never in our life style.

My daughter would always say that we had been poor her whole life. I tried to explain to her why we were in this condition. I would tell her that until I could get a better paying job we would be in this position. I told her that her father was not standing up to the plate by taking care of his daughter and this also contributed to our struggles. I also explained to her my opinion on the statement, "Be careful how you entertain strangers." To me this meant anyone not born into your family is considered a stranger. These strangers were the ones that GOD put in our path to help us, not my family but the strangers. So everyone who is not born into your family is considered a stranger and in most cases this is where your help will come from. This is why it pays to be nice to people. Treat them the way you want to be treated and GOD will allow it to come back to you. My daughter and I survived in the big city of Chicago without family or friends and most of the people that we did know. Strangers, not the people that we knew, but people that we didn't know, helped us along the way. Strangers feed us, clothed us and gave us cash.

I know what it is like to not having anything or having to beg people on the streets for quarters, it's called doing what you have to do. Everyone is not begging because they want drugs or alcohol, many are begging because they don't have family or any type of support system. I am not ashamed, I had to do what I had to do to survive. Ask and it shall be given. Everyone would always judge me but no one knew the situation that my daughter and I were in, they just judged me from the outside. Everyone thinks that if you don't look needy you don't need anything, but what does a needy person really look like?

In 2005 I was beyond tired. I was trying my best to keep my head above water and tired of begging my boss for an increase. I had already realized that this profession is not going to work for me because the cost of living expense was much too high to make it on such low salary. When I was married and had a second income I considered it enough. But it is all about survival here in Chicago and if you don't make enough money you will do without a lot of things or even be on the streets. I had come to the conclusion that I had to go back to school to change my career once again. I didn't have many years to waste because I was not getting any younger. I had already spent approximately four years in school to become a mortician and I made more money waiting tables than working as a mortician. When my boss told me that I was making top pay at thirteen dollars an hour I was devastated. I could not believe that after going to school for approximately four years to be a mortician plus my apprentice year, that thirteen dollars would be top pay. I had to leave my job or lose everything and go right back into the shelter starting over once again and I didn't want that to happen. My daughter had been doing without all of her life, not even having some of the simple things in life, and I didn't want her to continue her life like that.

I had to leave my job, not because I wanted to but because I was forced too. I left the best job that I have ever had in my life. I hated to leave my job but my boss didn't have a clue as to what I had to do, on a daily basis, to hold myself together. I felt that I was ripped from my passion and there was nothing I could do about it. I couldn't stay, I could not support my daughter and I on what I was making, so what was I suppose to do. Besides I was tired, my soul was tired, I walked away from my job on faith. I didn't have another job at the time but nothing from nothing leaves nothing. When I left my job my bank account was in a negative status and all my bills were due or passed due but I had to trust that GOD was going to work things out. I knew it was not going to be easy. I stepped out on faith once again, realizing that I had been stepping out and living by faith all my life.

Nothing about my life had been easy. I had already come to the conclusion that I had to stay in school and change my career once again. I had already spent approximately four years in school to become a mortician and I was making less money than waiting on tables. I still needed to continue my schooling. When I left my job I continued to go to school fulltime and I am presently still in school fulltime. My daughter said, "Mom we've been poor all my life." I told her that I knew it, and that her father was not pulling his side of the bargain. Seventy-four dollars every two weeks was only thirty-seven dollars a week and that was only if he paid. I went to the public aid office once again to see if I could get food stamps. I was not working and this time they politely told me that I did not qualify because I was going to school to get a higher degree. I was also disqualified because I did not have children under the age of six.

At the very end of 2005 out of the blue the child support division gave me a call from Springfield Illinois. They asked, "How has Maurice being getting away with the exact same amount for all those years?" I politely told them he had not gotten away but he had gotten by. And that because I had been in Chicago for the past ten years and he was in Springfield that my case always ended up in the files that people took their time to get around to. This was when the child support division decided to investigate my case. I was told that it would take a while but it didn't matter to me because at this point I had already waited ten years for any type of response from the child support division. I have had quite a life here in Chicago. It has been quite a challenge, but I had faith in GOD, that he was going to turn all of these things around to work for my good.

After my marriage with Erick I had decided to wait on GOD and to let Him do it. When Erick told me that GOD said I was going to be his wife, I should have known he was up to something because over the years I realized that GOD didn't tell me that Erick was going to be my husband. I don't know what was Erick's motive but I am sure during our marriage nothing went the way He thought it was going to go. I just thank GOD for letting Erick walk out of my life with the same thing that he came in with, his backpack. I thank

GOD that Erick walked away and didn't look back. People would ask me where is your husband and I would proudly say, with my head held high, "My husband left me." Everybody thought that we were just the perfect little family but people don't have a clue to what goes on behind closed doors. Never judge a book by the cover, you will be fooled every single time.

Finally, at the end of 2006 I got a letter from the child support division stating that I would be getting an increase in my child support starting January 2007. I knew this was GOD stepping in because for eleven years I had only received seventy-four dollars every two weeks (when he paid) and nothing extra. In January 2007 my daughter was approaching fifteen years old. She had been doing without since the age of two, when her father and I divorced. It always seems the kids are always the ones that suffer the most through divorce or separations. I had to struggle with my kids because I chose to do the right thing, to me ex meant ex so therefore I wasn't going to sneak around with them just to get them to take care of their children. I have to truly admit that Sam did step to the plate and take his son. He never asked me for a dime but if I had any extra money during my last marriage I would make sure that I sent my son something every month. However, Maurice on the other hand, abandoned his daughter when she was two years old, didn't start paying child support until she was almost four, and paid seventy-four every other week until she was fifteen years old. He really thinks that he took care of his daughter.

The support was raised in January 2007. Maurice tried to get it decreased because he said it was too much, and the judge told him that the law required twenty percent of his income and this was what he had to pay. The problem was his support jumped from thirty-seven dollars a week to one hundred forty-four dollars a week. This was a big jump for him so he told the judge that when he got her in the summer time he didn't want to pay child support and the judge agreed to that. At this point I knew, for next few years if nothing else, Maurice was going to be taking Kathyrn in the summer time because he didn't want to pay that amount of money for child support. He should have been taking his daughter every summer anyway. We had lived here for more than ten years, I thought the least he would do was take her every summer but that hardly ever happened. I thought he'd buy some school clothes too but I never got anything for my daughter. He missed out on so many years of her life, I just could not believe that a father would do such a thing. He had only been with her two summers out of all those years. What a shame that he missed out being in her life when she was younger. This affected my daughter in more ways than we can imagine. Maurice could not wait until the summer of 2007 to get his daughter. He would continually call to find out when she would be out of school for the summer. Summer could not come fast enough for Maurice because he didn't want to pay the child support. He still thought that that was too much money. Money was all that was ever on Maurice's mind not the child.

I took Kathyrn to Springfield in July of 2007 to spend the summer with her father and she poured out her heart to him about how we had been struggling all those years in Chicago and doing without, trying to make ends meet. My daughter was correct, because we had been struggling. Ever since she was two years old we have had to do without some of the simple things. I have never been able to get my kids anything for Christmas, birthdays, school clothes etc. I had to try to keep a roof over their heads but they always had my present with them. My kids and I have never had a Thanksgiving dinner or Christmas dinner together, I always had to try to keep shelter for us so extras never took place. My son was glad to go back to Springfield and live with his father because he said he was tired of struggling and not having nice things. My kids and I never had the pleasure of going shopping for new things, never. It was always about keeping a roof over their heads and there was never any extra money. I could not be mad at my son because if I had somewhere to run to I would have done the same thing. Therefore my daughter had it worse than he did. She had to struggle and do without all the years she was with me because there was only so much one can do with one income and with the cost of living the way it is in Chicago.

Once Kathyrn made it to Springfield she called me and told me she wanted to stay with her father because she was tired of struggling and doing without. I could not be mad at her because of her decision. Her father made it seem as though he cared so much and stated that he could do more for her than I was doing. He also said he didn't know that we were living under those conditions. I had told him that I was in school fulltime trying to get an education to better myself, therefore I didn't have a problem with him taking his daughter. He is her father. He also asked why didn't we tell him about all the struggles? He would have gotten her earlier. I knew this was not true because I remember her begging him to come and pick her up when she was in elementary school and we never heard from him. But as soon as the child support got raised, he got interested in her and wanted to take her so he would not have to pay me child support. It was like she never existed until he found time to fit her in. After Maurice had gotten all this information from his daughter, on how we were living and doing without necessary things that we needed to survive, I thought he would have a heart, considering that he was never there throughout all those years. He still doesn't have a clue as to what we had to go through in Chicago trying to survive.

I had taken Kathyrn to Springfield in July of 2007 and in September of 2007 I was hit was child support papers in the mail. I could not believe it! All those years he had done nothing besides sending the thirty-seven dollars a week whenever he did pay. How could a person have the heart to do something like that to the mother of his child? The one who had struggled with his child all those years without any additional help from anyone? Whatever is in that person's heart GOD will have to show us, and when He shows us believe Him because it is what it is.

I have been a fulltime struggling college student since 2005. It is 2009 and I am still a fulltime struggling college student but who cares. Completing college is a must for me and I can't let anyone stop me. Do you really think anyone cared that I have had to give up my second child because I could not afford to support and feed her on my own—the same reason I had to give up my first child? Of course not, who cares about that or who cares how I feel about that. I have learned in this society whether in or outside of the church that nobody cares until the shoe is on the other foot. This is okay too because as long as I have GOD I could care less what people think about me and what I had to do, because until you have actually walked in my shoes you cannot judge me. This is my journey. Everyone has their own journey and many don't live to tell their story. This could have been me but GOD knew already that I would live through it. I am just a nobody trying to tell anyone who will listen about how good GOD has been to me and how He has kept me on my journey. He allowed me to still be in my right mind through it all. Even though I felt alone for the past twenty-five years I have not been alone. GOD has been my mother, father, sister, brother, friend, doctor, lawyer, provider, way maker, and the list goes on and on. I don't have room to complain about anything that has happened in my life because GOD was with me. He was the one that stayed with me through it all and He never turned his back on me no matter what.

Chapter 6

Life with GOD

I arrived in Chicago in January 1997 and within six months I was homeless and had to send my son back to Springfield because I could not take care of him. I had to split my family, which consisted of me and my two kids, because I could not afford to take care and support both of them in Chicago. I told him my son I would come and get him in about a year once I got situated with my own place.

It was now January of 2009, approximately twelve years later and I have not been financially able, nor stable, to get my son and now my daughter is gone for the exact same reason. Throughout those twelve years there were many times I could not even go see him because I never had the money or could get the money. I have no regrets because I did what I felt was right to do. I could not take care of him or support him, and I felt that that was his father's responsibility if he could do it.

My son is now grown and has a family of his own. He now has fathered three children of his own. My daughter has been with her father for about a year and a half and I am sure that he can see that there is nothing easy about raising kids. He really needed to know this so he would have a clue of what my life was like, doing it all by myself in a big city like Chicago. I felt that my daughter needed to get to know her father, because the question that she asked me years ago stayed in the back of my mind. What would happen to her if something actually happen to me? You would think that being in a big city like Chicago for twelve years that someone would truly be in my corner, but not so.

I have had to truly lean and depend on no one but my GOD to make a way for me in all my situations. I found out that I didn't have real true friends because I was struggling to survive and no one offered to help. I have GOD and this is how I am able to hold my head up high and keep on traveling my journey. People come and go and in the end you have to ask yourself what did they really want anyway. They don't want to be friends they just want to know all the in and outs about your business and spread it on. Kathryn never knew my family and now she has gotten an opportunity to know her father and his family. I do realize that life is nothing but a journey and it was never promised that things were supposed to be easy, but things will be feasible. No one can tell you what lies ahead for we will just have to keep on walking the journey, trying our best to get to our final destination. There are many challenges, setbacks, roadblocks, etc. that life is full of, but as long as you keep on moving you will be making some kind of progress. However, we should remember that we can't change people and we can't make people do anything, so we should live our life and not worry about other people. There is a time and place for everything and I truly believe that things happen in our life exactly when they are supposed to happen, and there is nothing we can do about it. I will not and shall not complain because I can see that it was all in GOD's plan for my life. For this reason I should not grumble or complain because I am sure that things can always be worse than they are, have been, or can be. Everyone is walking his or her journey. Some think they are getting away with things but they are not, all they have to do is just keep walking and sooner or later they are going to run into what they thought they had gotten away from. This journey is so intense it can either make you or break you, and only the ones that want to survive will make it. In most cases the ones that dish it out can't take it when it comes back around.

I have been here in Chicago for twelve years now and I do know that it's only GOD's grace and mercy that is keeping me. I can truly say that I know why there are so many homeless people living here in such a big city. Everybody is not homeless because they might have a drug or alcohol problem. We should not be judged because we are needy or begging. Have you ever thought that many are homeless because no one, especially family, would give them a little helping hand? I can remember standing begging for quarters so I can relate, it is called "Doing what you have to do". We, as homeless people, especially if we don't know GOD, have to depend on the strangers. Many people will sit and listen to everyone's sad story but will not offer a dime or even give positive advice or just words of encouragement, which can go a long way. When people are in a needy struggling situation how could one have the heart to lend them money when they know needy means they can't pay it back? GOD put us here to help each other. People would be surprised how a smile, or just a kind word will make ones day. The worse thing a person can do is listen to you pour your heart out and turn around and say, "Let me know if you need anything." Those are the type people that are not going to help anyone. Five or ten dollars could do wonders in a struggling person's life. It took two dollars and feed me and my daughter. It is just truly amazing how I have spent twelve years of my life here, have met many people (so called friends) and no one has ever offered to feed me and my daughter, the whole twelve years that I have been faithful in the church, sad but it is true. When we go to church we are looking for Christ like people that actually mean what they say, but this is not always the case. I have to truly admit that I was expecting the people in the church to show love because I wasn't getting that in the streets or from family, but I was fooled once again.

I do realize that my GOD sees everything. Everyone that promised me something never got around to giving it to me. I take these as lessons of life, as experiences, and I've learned that one really doesn't have true friends. The best way to find out who your true friends are is to get sick, lose your job, or be struggling. They don't want to be in your company, they are so afraid you might ask them for something, but what they don't realize is that you have GOD and as long as you have GOD you will have every need met. GOD already knows the hearts of people and it is not even in most people's heart to do what is right. It is very sad to say but most of the people with the worst heart problems are sitting in the church. I have been faithfully in the church since I dedicated my life back to Christ in 1992. I've gone to weekly bible classes and church. Every Sunday GOD wakes me and gets me up. I have never in my life seen so many old jealous hearted people. You can't fool GOD's people they can see straight through you. It appears that many church folks have such madness in their hearts because of choices that they made, and they are mad at the world. Many feel that they have lived a long life and didn't do or get the opportunity to do what they wanted to do and now they want someone to blame. So What! Who's fault is that? If you have lived here on GOD's beautiful earth claiming you know how good GOD is and GOD has allowed you to live over fifty years or more why have you not made some type of accomplishment toward your goals? You pretend that you have been living for GOD. I don't understand that one. You have to search your heart and make sure you don't have blockage, which is being jealous against your fellowman. GOD judges everyone by their hearts not from what comes out of their mouth. GOD knows what is truly in one's heart, but one doesn't realize it shows what you are holding in your heart straight on your face. And they have the nerve to wonder why GOD has not answered some of their prayers. Heart problems means they have envy, strife, and jealousy in their hearts toward their neighbor without a cause. They don't realize that this journey is hard for everyone that is walking it, young and old, and there is no need to be jealous of your fellowman.

Everyone that is still living is on a journey. Each of us who have run to the church and who are either mentally or physically sick are the ones who are admitting that we need help. We run to the church because it is like the hospital, and we do need help because we are sick. The biggest problem that I have seen has been a bad heart problem for the majority of us, this is the reason many of us never get what we want in life. We all have to search our own heart daily. If GOD is not answering your prayers, it could be something that you are holding in your heart against your fellowman that is causing blockage. If you still can't even find a true friend (so-called saint) in the church, then that should tell you that you don't really have friends at all. So who's fooling who? Someone might wonder what does that have to do with my life story? Well older folks are supposed to be role models, because they are influences in one life and either you are going to want to follow in their footsteps or not. Most of them don't show any role models skills at all. They show madness and jealousy in their hearts, and who wants to be like that? The bible is the road-map to salvation and it teaches us how to live and if we are living by those guidelines why do we have so much madness in our hearts? I always was taught older people were supposed to set examples for younger people, where are they?

I have spent 20 years of my life in committed abusive relationships and I gave my all to make things work. Being a battered woman for half my life has changed my whole life. For the woman that is quick to say she is not being abused, mental abuse is worse than physical abuse. I have had a dinner (taste) of both types of abuse. Women please wake up. If your man truly loves you he will not abuse you. Fortunately after 20 long years I am still alive and in my right mind, I owe it all to GOD. After of all the bruises, black eyes, heartaches, blows to head, doctor visits, and all, I realized that if it wasn't for GOD I would not have lived to tell my story. I feel domestic violence takes place in a majority of all relationships and some women are not even aware of it. I have learned many lessons when it comes to men. First of all, if he didn't love GOD it was impossible for him to love me. GOD did not create women to be used, abused, or treated like slaves by our spouses or companions. We are not punching bags, not by no means. When men are abusive they don't love themselves so it is impossible for them to even know how to love us. I have had things done to me that I would not do to a dog, but even though they happened GOD allowed me to live through it all. Being in an abusive relationship is something that one will never forget, but through the grace of GOD women can live on and have a prosperous life. Although I have never ever been truly loved by any man I still believe that GOD will have a special man come into my life, one who is willing to accept me just the way I am. I realize that GOD truly loves me no matter what.

We women have to stop settling for less, but if we don't stand for something we will fall for anyone or anything. Life is wonderful and meant to be lived to the fullest but as long as we continue to be in abusive domestic violence relationships and think that it is okay, we will never exceed to our greatest potential. I believe that every woman that is married or has been married or in a committed relationship has the same story, unless her spouse loves GOD first. If her spouse or companion doesn't love GOD, guess what, he won't love you because he doesn't know how and you are just fooling yourself if you think he does. I am sure you have a story to tell as well. It does not matter if you have been married two years or forty years, if your marriage has not lined up according to the word of GOD and GOD's guidelines you have gone through unnecessary drama. For this reason many women have madness in their hearts looking for someone to blame other than themselves. When you decide to own up to your bad choices the same way that I did, you can have the peace that GOD has left for everyone to endure. But you have to be able to see what part you played in your own situation and realize that nobody made you do anything. We do things because we want to and the bottom line is maybe it was just the lust of your flesh as well, if you didn't do it GOD's way. This makes us no different from anyone else, young or old — if you don't follow the guidelines that GOD gave us to follow when it comes to your mate, then yes, you are just dealing with the consequences that comes with disobedience. But GOD's grace and mercy has kept you in your right mind for twenty, thirty, forty, years etc. It was not anything special that you did, it was GOD grace and mercy.

If older women would open up and share their story it would truly help younger women do the right thing. So I made it my business to tell my story because I am not ashamed of what I went through, and if telling my story can touch one woman's heart, I am glad about it. We are human and we make mistakes. People need to know this so they will understand how to deal with these issues, ones that most women are faced with. If you are in an abusive relationship stop lying about your journey. Your face shows that your journey has been intense. The truth will not only set you free but may also help someone else understand that they are not alone in whatever it is that they are going through. I do believe that if there had been an older woman who shared her story, and was honest about it, there are some things that I might not have done. There are no secrets in life and nothing is new, so tell your story, let women know what their value is. What better person to hear this from than a seasoned woman who has already been there and done that. But the seasoned women are so afraid to tell it because now they are in church perpetrating to be perfect women, and we know perfect women don't exist. Just tell it, I guarantee you it will touch someone's heart and they will listen and not want to make the same mistakes. This is what I thought the older women in the church were there for but it appears that I was wrong. Older women look as this as telling their business, but everyone who have been married or in a relationship already knows what you have to go through, so it is not a secret, tell it. Don't just tell the good, we need to hear the good, the bad, and the ugly. Besides what are you ashamed of, once you become truly saved it is past tense. This is the reason I am not ashamed to tell my story and the unwise choices that I made in my life. No one made me do it, I did it because I wanted to do and it was the lust of my flesh, now I can move on with my life and enjoy GOD's peace that He has left here for me.

To All The Single Ladies
Who Want To Live A Better Life

I have learned so much during the last twenty-five years of my life and especially the years that I have been divorced and single. I've learned that if he is not a real man, or he is not the one for you and you should leave him alone if he:

» doesn't have anything to offer you other than going to bed.

» doesn't have goals and dreams that you can be a part of.

» never takes you to his place or meet his parents.

» is willing to bed but not to wed.

» not willing to help you in any kind of way.

» does not work and wants you to support him.

» only tells you his name and where he works.

» is not willing to get to really know you.

» only calls to take you out to the club a nice date.

» does not have a steady job, his own place, or transportation, so you have to ask yourself what does he want with you.

» has to be intoxicated every time you all go on a date

» continues to go to bed with you and does absolutely nothing else for you

» can't see that you are a beautiful queen, inside and out.

God created us to be loved, to be treated with dignity and respected. If we are not getting this, we are missing out on GOD's goodness that he has promised us. Men treat women the way they wanted to be treated but boys—all they want to do is play and never pay. They want something for nothing. Why keep giving them everything that we own and getting nothing in return but disappointment and humiliation. Ladies don't continue to get cheated out of the simple things in life that mean the most such as, respect, intimacy, a shoulder to cry on, best friends, someone to confide in and trust, compliments, encouragements, and last but not least someone to walk by your side (not in front or behind you). I spent twenty years of my life with three different men and never had anyone to talk to nor a shoulder to cry on but thank GOD I woke up while I am still young and realized that I have cheated myself for half of my life. I don't know what it is like to be with a real man, have someone to talk too, a shoulder to cry on, or someone just to hold my hand. I have a lot to look forward to during the second half of my life. I have spent my whole life alone but GOD has given me the opportunity to start over and get it right this time. In order to do that and get the best that GOD has for me I have to let him do it and do his way. GOD allowed me to live through all types of abuse and domestic violence from men that should have damage me for life but through GOD's grace and mercy they hurt my body but they couldn't touch my soul. Through all those years that I spent with three different men, I can truly say I don't miss anything about them. I can't miss what I have never had, true love and someone to love me just the way that I am.

I know men tell us they love us all the time but deep down inside we know that is not true. Most of them don't even know the meaning of love and furthermore they don't even love themselves. So how can they love us? Why continue living a lie knowing that we are only here on earth for a short while? Nothing changes until we decide to change, once we change everything and everyone around us changes.

I have been on my own for twenty-five years now and I can honestly say that the only true friend that I have ever had in my entire life was my mother. There were times when I felt like everything was taken away from me. I may never have had true friends in my life or family but I realized that GOD was with me all the time and still is. True friends do not betray you, true friends stick together no matter what, true friends can accept your accomplishments and not be jealous, true friends can hear your cry, true friends want the best for you and most of all true friends will love you just for who you are and not try and change you. True friends do not talk about you behind your back. True friends will know that if they have a job and are still struggling then you have to be struggling because you're not working. It takes the same amount of money for us to get the same necessities in life. If your true friends do not fit this profile, maybe they are not really your true friends. I thank GOD for allowing me to be in a position to show me that I really didn't have true friends. Normally you find out who your true friends are if you don't have a job, don't have money, are sick, etc. These are just a few examples that really lets you know who is really in your corner. If you have never been in one of those positions you probably may still think you have many friends, but just keep walking the journey and you will see exactly how much you count. I believe if people can't fool or use you they really don't care to be around you. People don't realize that what is in their heart not only shows on their face but it comes out of their mouth as well.

For 20 years of my life while in those committed relationships I realized that I was mentally alone, the entire 20 years. It took the last six years for me to realize and be able to see that a lot of choices that I had made contributed to the different situations that I had to go through. I have been single for the last six years since my last divorce and I have realized that I am somebody, I love myself, I am beautiful inside out, and I can do all things through Christ who strengthens me. I have learned to keep GOD first and let him do it His way. This eliminates all the unnecessary situations of life that we don't have to endure. I truly believe that one day GOD will allow me to be happily married. I have enough wisdom and knowledge to know that I have to do it GOD's way and let Him do it because this is a job that is much too hard for me.

In the meantime I am continuing to reach toward my goals something that for years of my life I thought I would never get an opportunity to do. I felt as though my life was taken and everything was ripped from me but today I can truly say I have a lot to live for and be thankful for. Those twenty-five years have made me the woman that I am today. I know some things I might have brought on myself by making bad choices but I had to go through some of the things to know exactly what I am worth. We have to love ourselves regardless of how GOD has created us. We all are different, made differently, and think differently so we should not player hate on each other. GOD created us, we didn't created ourselves, so embrace the person you see in the mirror. If there is something in your life that you can change, then change it, but if you can't change it then you know that this is the way that GOD meant for it to be.

I am truly looking forward to the next half of my life being the greatest years of my life, living my life to the fullest and being the best that I can be in whatever I decide to do or accomplish. I was always abused but I was never refused by GOD. He accepted me just the way I was and He will get all the GLORY out of my life. Whatever GOD has for me it is for me and no one else can take it. I was abused, abandoned and yes I am still standing by the grace of GOD. I will continue to treat people the way I want to be treated. Also, I'm keeping GOD first in my life because I already know without him I am nothing and can't make it on my own.

To all my enemies who encouraged me to write this book years ago, I took your advice, now you can read my story. I also would like to thank you all for not helping me alone the way because I realize that it was meant for GOD to get the GLORY out of my life and not you. Always thank GOD for your enemies and your so-called friends because of them we are the people that we are today. After all those years and life lessons I can truly say that Jesus is the best thing that has ever happen to me. The Best is yet to come. My journey has been quite a lonely one but that just lets me know that I am doing something right. Anytime you are willing to stand for what is right in most cases you will be standing alone, but that's okay. GOD has that special person for everyone but it is in his timing. I don't like dealing with fickle, phony people because my life is too short and they just slow up my process. I don't care to be in the presence of someone who doesn't have time for me or just wants to see what they can get out of me. People like that don't make it far in life. First of all they don't realize that you can't fool people you only fool yourself, and in the end we all will have to stand before GOD and answer to everything that we done, right or wrong. Nobody gets away, they just get by for a moment, then GOD has to let them know that he is the captain of the ship. We have to always remember GOD sees and hears everything. If you have done anything wrong it is on record so don't think that you have gotten over on anyone, just wait, your turn is coming.

Conclusion

Our journey is such a mystery, meaning that we will never know what we will have to face in life but we should always remember it could be worse. Each of us has to walk out on our own journey and no one can do it for us. The key for me is that regardless of what I went through I still found in my heart to treat people the way I wanted to be treated, even when I didn't feel like it, and even when I knew they thought they were taking advantage of me and thought I didn't know any better. Whatever is done in the dark, whether good or bad, will come to the light. I knew they were only hurting themselves because they didn't know me anyway. I always knew that someday things would change because nothing remains the same and no one gets away with anything, they only get by until the time is right.

I was also able to realize that walking in GOD's favor gave me more than money could ever buy. Although my heart has been ripped out and broken many times, over and over again throughout my life, GOD had a way of making all those heart breaks work out in my favor. As long as I put GOD first in my life and do what I am suppose to do the sky is the limit. I have learned to let GOD place people in my life because not just anybody will understand where GOD is taking me, and there is no room for player haters because haters go to hell. I've learned to encourage myself and strive for the best. There are very few true friends, if any, so if anyone has real friends you better hold on to them. If they are not true friends GOD will surely let you know. I know everyone has their own story to tell but I just thank GOD every day that he let me live to tell mine, because there were many times I thought I would never live to be the age that I am now. We will all have trials and tribulations but how we deal with them makes all the different in the world. If everyone took their eyes off of people and placed their eyes on

GOD I guaranteed you the journey would not seem as bad as they thought it was. It if doesn't kill you it will surely make you strong and this is the purpose of life trials and tribulations. Search your heart, don't be jealous of other people, everyone is created just the way GOD wanted them to be so embrace yourself. You can't change anyone, only GOD can do that. Everything that GOD has for everyone has our name is on it so stop being jealous of your fellowman. Whatever GOD has for you is for you and no one can take it from you no matter how they try.

Last but not least, if you are still confused about why you are here on earth and don't know what GOD wants you to do try helping someone on their journey before you get to the end of your journey, I promise you that you will need some help from someone along the way too. Always remember that whatever you give out will come back to you. We all have heard that what goes around comes back around to you. This is how GOD allowed me to make it throughout my life without my family and any so-called friends, I always treated people the way that I wanted to be treated and gave when I had it to give, so all I had to do was ask and it was given back to me. No amount of money or no person can take the place of walking in GOD's favor. Please always remember to be careful how you entertain strangers. I was a stranger in the city of Chicago, so everyone that actually came across my path didn't have any evidence of who I really was. They didn't have a clue that I was just a stranger on a mission for GOD and this was the reason I was misused and mistreated. But I do know it has been well worth the trip knowing that GOD was on my side all the time, doing for me what I could not do for myself. And through it all GOD will continue to get the glory in every area of my life and GOD will not allow anyone to share his Glory with him.

To all the men who came across my path and thought I was a fool, always remember a fool can't fool a fool. Meaning, if your name does not appear in my book, you didn't MEAN anything to me either.

ALWAYS BE CAREFUL HOW YOU TREAT A STRANGER

To all the men and women who crossed my path and met me, it is time to be honest with yourself and set yourself free. Take the time to search deep within your hearts and ask yourself this million dollar question. "What did Ruby ever do to me to deserve to be treated the way I treated her?"

THANK YOU JESUS FOR DELIVERING ME FROM PEOPLE

I am just a stranger, trying to tell anyone who will listen, how good my GOD has been to me. He can do the same thing for you if you allow Him too.

www.ingramcontent.com/pod-product-compliance
Lightning Source LLC
Chambersburg PA
CBHW072209090426

42740CB00012B/2450